Horse
Racing
Manual

First published in March 2018

A catalogue record for this book is available from the British Library.

ISBN 978 1 78521 169 0

Library of Congress control no. 2017949623

Published by Haynes Publishing,
Sparkford, Yeovil, Somerset BA22 7JJ, UK.
Tel: 01963 440635
Int. tel: +44 1963 440635
Website: www.haynes.com

Haynes North America Inc.,
859 Lawrence Drive, Newbury Park,
California 91320, USA.

Printed in Malaysia.

AUTHOR ACKNOWLEDGEMENTS

There are many aspects to racing and covering them all properly in the course of writing this book has required some expert help. I would firstly like to extend my professional thanks to Louise McIntyre of Haynes and photographer Tracy Roberts, but also to many others for their time, patience and information.

Those I have not mentioned in writing or credited in pictures include Charlie Vigors, sales consigner of Hillwood Stud, as well as trainers Michael Attwater, Marcus Tregoning, Noel Williams, Jim Boyle and Ben Pauling. I also owe a debt of gratitude to Jason Singh of Tattersalls, Robin Mounsey, Joe Rendall and Peter Hobbs from the British Horseracing Authority, Hattie Lawrence of the Valley Equine Hospital and Helen Gale from Rossdales in Newmarket for explaining equine health issues, Jayne Matthews and Jackie Porter at Oaksey House, equine behavioural expert Gary Witheford, Chapel Forge Farriers, Sinead Hyland, Ian Lawrence, Hayley Moore, Harriet Collins, Emma Berry, Kate Hills, Edward Prosser, James McHale, Marcus Armytage, Richard Hayler and Andrew Griffiths. Last, but no means least, I had better thank my parents James and Harriet Peacock for their suggestions and eagle-eyed sub-editing.

Author	Tom Peacock
Editor	Louise McIntyre
Page design	James Robertson
Photographer	Tracy Roberts (TurfPix.com)

Horse Racing Manual

The in-depth guide to owning, training, racing and following

Tom Peacock
Foreword by Paul Nicholls

Contents

◀ Three-times Cheltenham Gold Cup
winner Best Mate on the gallops

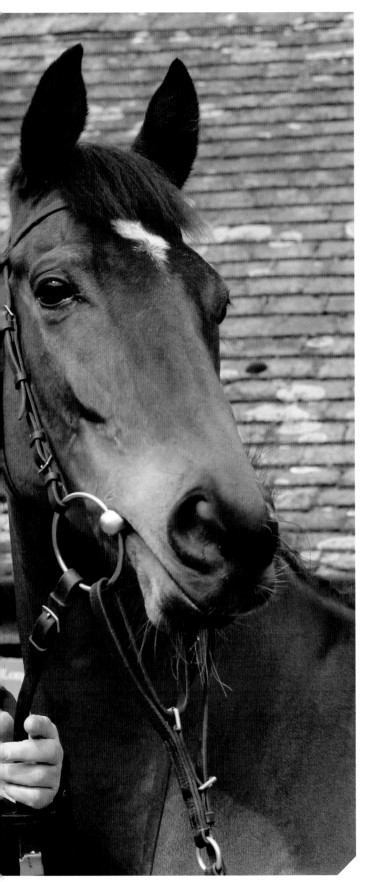

Foreword

Brought up just outside Bristol and from a family of policemen, Paul Nicholls had a relatively successful career as a jump jockey, twice winning the Hennessy Gold Cup at Newbury. It is as a trainer that he has really excelled, from growing his stable in the village of Ditcheat in Somerset from just a handful of horses in 1991 to collecting multiple championships and all of the major prizes including the Grand National.

My granddad first got me into racing. He used to like having a bet and watching it on the television. I was only about six but I just got hooked on it, eventually persuading my dad to buy me a pony as I thought I might like to become a jockey.

I still love the sport as much as ever, and I love the people. The first thing my great friend and landlord Paul Barber said to me when I began training was 'delegate, my boy, delegate, and then you'll be fine'. You have to let people get on and do their job. We can have 125 horses at any one time in training and more than 50 staff and luckily I've got a brilliant team, from my head lad and assistants to the lads and lasses and my team in the office. We call it 'Team Ditcheat', as we want to make everyone feel part of a team and involved in the whole package. For owners, it should not just be about writing a cheque and having one horse with us; at the end of the day it's a hobby for people and it's all about enjoyment.

I've been very lucky to train some brilliant horses such as See More Business, Kauto Star and Denman, but you've got to just keep finding the next generation of them. Winners are what motivate me – whether it's a lowly race at Taunton or Newton Abbot or the Cheltenham Gold Cup. You're only as good as your last winner.

You have to get used to dealing with the stressful parts of the job, but when I get into the yard at a quarter past six with everyone, sorting out what we're riding and what's running, watching them jumping and progressing from A to B, it's still just awesome.

Paul Nicholls

Introduction

With annual crowds of nearly six million people, horse racing is Britain's second most-attended sport behind only football. It is also truly global, with major events held everywhere from the party of the Melbourne Cup in Australia to the colossal Meydan racecourse in Dubai, all across the Americas and Asia to a meeting on the beach at Laytown in Ireland.

The attractions are manifold. Racehorses themselves are beautiful creatures capable of reaching speeds of 40 miles per hour through centuries of refined breeding. It has always been glamorous, attracting every section of society from kings and queens downwards. Surveys have found it has a far higher female customer base than the average for other major sports. A crucial pull-factor is that everyone can be engaged with it at some level. You might be a spectator at a fixture, have an interest in horses and riding, or just fancy an occasional betting flutter.

It is also not only about being at marquee occasions such as Royal Ascot or the Cheltenham Festival, as there is always a meeting to follow somewhere. With around 14,000 racehorses that need looking after in Britain, horse racing is a significant employer and is covered regularly by newspapers and national television. British Horseracing Authority figures estimate that the industry is worth over £3.45 billion annually to the national economy, supplying 85,000 direct and indirect full-time jobs. There are more than 8,000 horses trained in Ireland, where racing is an even more integral part of daily life.

Whilst for many the appeal of racing is its sophistication, the mystique of it can be disorienting or even off-putting to a newcomer. Far more than simply the premise of one horse running faster than all of the rest it is built on old-fashioned language, which it is assumed everyone will instantly understand. But where do the horses come from? Why do some of them jump over fences? What do all of those words and numbers used by bookmakers even mean? This is all before you have even tried to have a bet, let alone buy a horse yourself.

Hopefully this book will answer all of those questions and more, leaving the reader armed with enough useful information to get more out of their days at the races. The uninitiated need not worry, though. Even racing professionals never stop learning something new about this consuming sport.

Tom Peacock

The world of horse racing

Horse racing comes in a few different varieties, although the premise is the same, with the fastest, luckiest or most determined horse passing the winning post first. Whilst the modern sport developed from riders and horses competing against each other along a long flat course, it gradually branched into events over different distances and jumps began to be incorporated. In recent times, artificial surfaces have sometimes been used instead of the traditional grass. Most organised competition involves the Thoroughbred horse, but this is not exclusively so.

The history of horse racing

There has been evidence of horse racing since ancient times in Greece and the Middle East, spreading into popularity amongst the Romans, not only with *Ben-Hur*-style chariot competitions but also with horses being ridden by jockeys.

This form of entertainment, however, would be very different to the form of racing we see today. The development of the modern version is generally considered to have begun in 17th-century England and encouraged by King Charles II, a genial and high-spirited monarch who liked to spend his leisure time in Newmarket. He conceived, rode in and won the Newmarket Town Plate, a race that still exists in a form today on a course at the small market town on the Cambridgeshire/Suffolk border. Newmarket has always been regarded as the sport's spiritual home as well as its epicentre.

The oldest organised races were usually matches between two Thoroughbred horses over long distances and were certainly not a mass spectator sport – and indeed the hoi polloi were often actively discouraged. These were private battles between the aristocracy to see whose animal was best, although a wager or two might well take place on the side.

By the 19th century, racing was becoming far more popular, by which time many of today's most famous races such as the 2000 Guineas and the Derby had been established, and a crowd of 100,000 assembled to see 'The Great Match' between The Flying Dutchman and Voltigeur at York in 1851. British influence saw the sport successfully introduced into Ireland, France, Australia, America and even Japan.

From a hobby for the wealthy or races between amateurs,

2016'S MOST-ATTENDED BRITISH SPORTING EVENTS

(Source: event organisers, Deloitte analysis)

Event	Attendance	Duration
Wimbledon Tennis Championships	494,000	(14 days)
F1 British Grand Prix	327,000	(3 days)
Royal Ascot	295,000	(5 days)
Cheltenham Festival	261,000	(4 days)
ATP World Tennis Finals	252,000	(8 days)
The Open Golf Championship	173,000	(8 days)
Badminton Horse Trials	160,000	(5 days)
Moto GP Silverstone	156,000	(3 days)
Burghley Horse Trials	155,000	(4 days)
Epsom Derby	154,000	(2 days)

horse racing has morphed into a professional behemoth in which millions are at stake. Modern-day racing has had to become more tightly controlled in order to preserve its integrity and the governance of the British Horseracing Authority (BHA) and other such international bodies is designed to provide this.

Far more recent innovations include the use of starting stalls, racecourse commentators, photo finish technology and random drug testing.

▼ **The Flying Dutchman and Voltigeur running The Great Match At York Racecourse** *(Getty Images)*

Types of racing

Flat racing

Much the most prevalent form of racing around the world, the Flat is the traditional summer pursuit and is often also known as 'the Turf', because it is staged on grass. The proper season across Europe starts around March and runs until the end of November, although it is year-round in many countries.

Flat racing, as ought to be self-explanatory, does not incorporate jumping obstacles. The horses are bred for speed and race over distances between five furlongs (with one furlong equalling 200m) and around two miles. Like human athletes, some horses are better at shorter and some at longer events. The horse's optimum distance usually depends upon its 'pedigree' – in other words, the distances over which its parents and grandparents excelled – but this is not a hard and fast rule.

Races are started using stalls, devised in the interest of fairness so everyone gets a level break. In sprint races, runners tend to go hell-for-leather from the outset, whilst longer-distance events can become much more tactical.

Flat horses almost always begin their careers at two years old over short distances, a period in which they are still growing and developing physically. The most important time of their lives is at three, when a select few will be capable of running in the 'Classics'. The Classics start with the Guineas at Newmarket over a mile in the spring (one for males and one for females), moving up to a mile and a half for the Derby at Epsom in the summer, before the St Leger at Doncaster in the autumn at a mile and three-quarters. The races, which have all been staged for more than two centuries, are designed to find an ultimate champion with speed and stamina, and have been replicated around the world.

The Flat is the most lucrative and international side of racing. The very best horses can travel the world and earn prize money

▼ **Flat racing is a fast-moving sport of often tight margins**

that would impress even the super-rich, but greater value still lies in their breeding. Superstars can be whisked off to stud after only a few races rather than risking injury. Wealthy owners the world over want to have a champion and there is a far better chance of unearthing one if it has the right pedigree. Millions of pounds are spent on equine lottery tickets at horse sales each year in this pursuit.

An ordinary horse can continue racing at least a few times a year until they are eight or nine, but it is quite possible for a Flat horse to still be running into its teenage years.

Jump racing

Although jump racing takes place throughout the year, the core of its season and the time of the major events runs from early winter until the spring.

Jumping is a far newer sport than Flat racing, and its roots come from fox hunting. It is thought that the first recorded race was in 1752 in County Cork in Ireland, when two gentlemen took each other on through four miles of countryside, racing between the steeples of two village churches and coining the modern phrase 'steeplechase'.

It was not until the 19th century that jump racing, or 'National Hunt' racing, began to take place on organised tracks. Nowadays, the minimum distance for races is two miles,

WORLD'S RICHEST RACES IN 2017	
Pegasus World Cup, America	$12 million
Dubai World Cup	$10 million
Breeders' Cup Classic, America (venue changes annually)	$6 million
Prix de l'Arc de Triomphe, France	€5 million
Japan Cup	$5.7 million
Melbourne Cup, Australia	$5 million

stretching all the way to over four and a quarter miles for the Grand National at Aintree, the world's most famous jumping event. Many of the best-known racecourses, such as Ascot and Newbury, host both forms of the sport.

France, Britain and Ireland are by far the most important jumping nations, although it continues as something of a minority sport in other parts of Europe, America and Australasia. The Cheltenham Festival each March is jumping's showpiece, encouraging fierce but friendly competition between the chief British and Irish contenders. The Gold Cup is the purists' race

▼ **The Cheltenham Gold Cup is the most prestigious of jumping's prizes**

MOST VALUABLE JUMPS RACES IN 2017

Grand National, Britain	£1 million
Nakayama Grand Jump, Japan	$1.25 million
Grand Steeple-Chase de Paris	€850,000
Cheltenham Gold Cup, Britain	£575,000
Irish Grand National	€500,000

and the one every competitor dreams of winning.

Some Flat horses become jumpers, but most are bred for it specifically. Jumps horses are usually larger and more robust than their Flat counterparts. The riders are also able to be slightly bigger; instead of an average riding weight of between 8st and 9st, jump jockeys will be around the 10st mark.

Horses begin by running over smaller obstacles in hurdle races and can develop into specialists at that particular discipline. Others will later graduate to steeplechase fences and it is generally perceived that a jumping-bred horse, which takes far longer to mature than its Flat cousin, will be reaching its peak at the age of eight or nine.

▼ **The all-weather track at Lingfield** *(Arena Racing Company)*

Jumping does not have the financial value of the Flat, either in its races or through the breeding business, and the atmosphere tends to be more informal and relaxed. Perhaps due to the need to continue through inclement winter weather, it tends to draw the most ardent fans.

All-weather racing

By far the newest form of racing, all-weather racing was first introduced in Britain in 1989. It was felt that too many meetings were being lost due to wintry conditions and there was a need to plug the financial hole caused by lost betting revenue to the sport and the government on blank racing days. Instead of racing on grass, horses run on a synthetic surface. They are less susceptible to freezing in cold weather and horses cannot be risked on hard ground for fear that they will damage their joints and legs.

From the first two tracks at Lingfield in Surrey and Southwell in Nottinghamshire, there are now half a dozen all-weather venues in Britain and they have cropped up in France, Ireland and across the rest of the world. They are not all uniform, and are made from a variety of materials.

Whilst all-weather tracks should all theoretically be far lower-maintenance than grass, they do require regular harrowing and rotavating. It would cost at least £1m to replace an entire all-weather surface, but if looked after, they can last for many years.

Owing to concerns with safety, there is no longer any jump racing on all-weather tracks. The bulk of the all-weather meetings take place in the months when there is no grass racing, but they are still used year-round. All-weather racing is the least glamorous version of the sport with low-grade horses running in front of sparsely populated grandstands. However, promising young horses can sometimes take their first public steps at such meetings and a valuable event on Good Friday at Lingfield has become a popular occasion on the calendar.

All-weather racing is not the same as dirt racing, the surface that is used for most major events in America. Dirt mostly consists of sand combined with some clay and silt, and tends to only favour horses whose ancestors were suited to it.

Other types of racing

Point-to-point racing

Going to a point-to-point is practically identical to going jump racing, only with a feeling of stepping back in time. They started off as the same thing – that first race staged in Ireland between steeples was also described as running 'point to point' – but as the sport became more organised at the start of the last century it became something in its own right.

Point-to-point racing is essentially jump racing for amateur riders, instead of professionals, and rather than on racecourses with permanent infrastructure, most take place in fields or open countryside. Point-to-pointing is well regulated; riders must be insured, horses registered, and there is a set of rules similar to the jumps. You can even bet on it. The main qualification for each horse to run is that someone who is a member of a recognised hunt must own it.

▼ Point-to-point racing has its roots in hunting

There are more than 100 racecourses and 200 fixtures taking place between the winter and spring in Britain and half as many again in Ireland, set within some stunning rural landscapes. The sport is informal, accessible and inexpensive to attend, with picnicking encouraged. Just remember to be prepared for the weather and, nearly always, the muddy roads getting in and out.

By and large, the standard is lower. Many of the horses have either failed to make the grade in recognised jump racing or are in the twilight of their careers, and the riders and trainers are doing it for fun. However, the opposite can be true and it is regularly used to educate young horses that go on to better things. It can also be a good training ground for riders (British champion jockey Richard Johnson started his career in the division).

There are usually at least six races, nearly all three miles long, and over slightly smaller fences than those used in regular jump racing. Meetings will often also have a series of pony races for fearless children, a funfair and various country demonstrations. Despite the enforcement of a ban on fox hunting in 2005, hunt membership and point-to-pointing attendances have remained buoyant.

▼ Richard Johnson started in point-to-points and later became a champion jump jockey

Pointing received a welcome publicity boost in 2015 when British Olympic cycling gold medallist Victoria Pendleton took it up as part of a challenge to learn to ride competitively from scratch within a year.

Arabian racing

This is exactly the same as Flat racing, only with different horses. An ancient breed, Arabian horses existed thousands of years before the modern-day Thoroughbred used for racing. As a symbol of their homeland, Arabian racing has been promoted in Europe almost exclusively by the Middle East. Many of the sheikhs of the United Arab Emirates and Qatar who have Thoroughbreds trained in Europe are just as passionate about their Arabians.

A large handful of races held during the summer months are dotted around regular British, French and American tracks, either as events in their own right or added into regular race meetings. There are also valuable events held back in the Gulf.

It is very much a minority sport, which has only been properly organised in Britain since the early 1980s, with a few small 'hobby' trainers attempting to compete against the powerful Middle-Eastern backed practitioners. Few people probably know it goes on in Britain or even notice the difference between the horses straight away.

Nonetheless, all-Arabian meetings are usually inexpensive to attend and can be eventful. The horses are smaller than their more familiar contemporaries, with a shorter neck and stride, as well as being considered particularly intelligent as a breed. The Arabian is far more of a challenge to ride and train, as they will often do exactly what they want to do, rather than what is being asked of them. Note that they have a distinctive concave head, an arched neck and what can be a bit of a temper.

Quarter Horse racing

You are very unlikely to encounter racing with Quarter Horses in Europe. However, it is seen widely across North and Latin America. The horses are related to both the Thoroughbred and the Arabian but are their own distinct breed. They are a little smaller and more compact, and the biggest difference is their speed. The Quarter Horse is the equine drag racer, competing in only Flat races over very short distances. Many are over only 440 yards or two furlongs, which they can complete in around 20 seconds. California, Texas and New Mexico are the big Quarter Horse states and there are some valuable prizes, even if the sport does not attract quite the same mainstream attention of Thoroughbreds and some of the most successful human practitioners have ended up switching codes.

▶ Top-class Arabian horses battle out the finish to the valuable Kahayla Classic at Meydan in Dubai (Andrew Watkins/Dubai Racing Club)

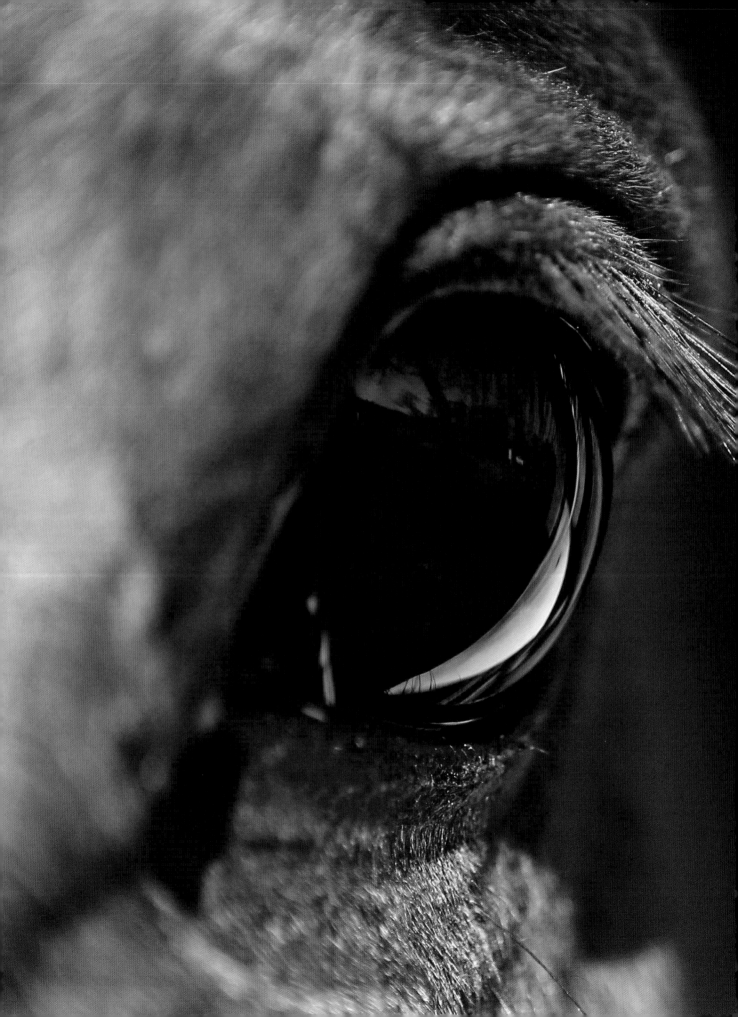

All Flat horses belong to a distinct breed known as the Thoroughbred, which can be traced back to the turn of the 18th century in Britain. Before that time, domestic breeds of horses were used for racing but everything changed with the arrival of horses from the regions of Syria and Yemen, which were first brought back as presents for the nobility.

The more lightly built Arabian stallions, famed for their remarkable ability to gallop through the desert, were bred with English mares to create a hybrid creature with speed and stamina. The Thoroughbred has an aristocratic head, an athletic body with long limbs and neck, and is perfectly designed for racing.

It is believed that virtually every racehorse can be traced back to one of three of these stallions – the Byerley Turk, the Godolphin Barb and the Darley Arabian, with the latter's blood reportedly present in 95% of those horses around today.

The racing authorities keep records of every Thoroughbred foal born in Britain and Ireland in what is known as the General Stud Book – a practice replicated around the world – so that the horses can be registered to race.

While a Thoroughbred is, in essence, inbred, as nearly every horse is related to each other, it is important that the families are not too close. Pedigree analysts are employed to find appropriate matches and stallions move nationally and internationally to freshen up the pool.

It is much the same case for jump racing, although the breeding is not as restrictive and certainly in the more casual times of the last century, some jump racehorses would have been related to hunting horses.

The majority of jumpers are bred in Ireland, but in recent years more precocious French horses have been brought across the Channel. Some of these are not pure Thoroughbreds but related to Anglo-Arabians or Selle Francais, other breeds that were developed for their capability in riding sports such as showjumping or eventing.

NORTHERN DANCER

This diminutive Canadian-bred horse, who won both the prestigious Kentucky Derby and Preakness in 1964, must be considered just as important to the whole Flat racing Thoroughbred as the Arabian founding fathers.

Northern Dancer made a fine start with his first offspring to race, but what was more impressive was that his children, too, became the most successful stallions.

Thanks to the likes of Danzig, Sadler's Wells and Storm Bird, his genes continued and the majority of horses that run in a major Derby can be traced back to him.

▼ Northern Dancer hits the finish line a neck ahead of Hill Rise, winning the Kentucky Derby (Getty Images)

Physique of the racehorse

The Thoroughbred racehorse has evolved over centuries of breeding into the perfect machine for running at speed. They are lean and athletic, with long legs and neck, a deep chest to house the lungs and heart, and powerful hindquarters to drive them along. The Thoroughbred is known as an intelligent breed and has always been around humans, meaning that they should theoretically be easy to look after, but the spirit and energy of most means that they are not recommended as riding horses for the complete beginner.

RACEHORSE FACTS

- A racehorse will usually weigh half a ton (1,000lb/ over 450kg).
- At full gallop it will pump 230 litres of blood around its body and take in 1,800 litres of air per minute.
- It can only breathe through its nose and in synch with its stride.
- Its heart is about 1% of its bodyweight. The heart will beat around 40 times per minute at rest and more than 200 times when galloping.
- It has more than 700 muscles, forming up to 55% of its body mass.
- Its brain weighs half that of a human.
- Its average lifespan is 25 years.
- Its ears can rotate 180 degrees.

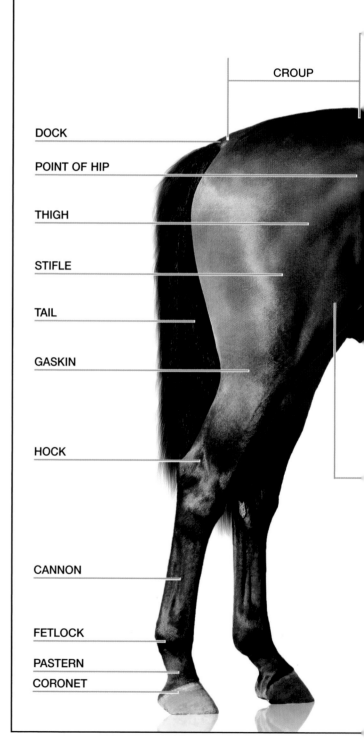

CROUP

DOCK

POINT OF HIP

THIGH

STIFLE

TAIL

GASKIN

HOCK

CANNON

FETLOCK

PASTERN

CORONET

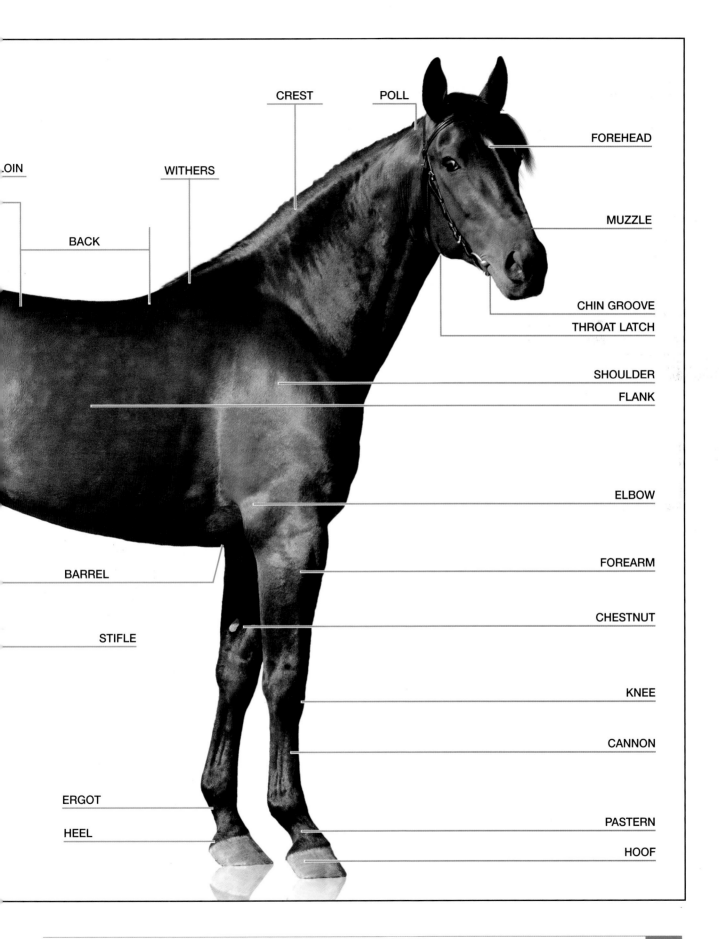

CREST

POLL

FOREHEAD

LOIN

WITHERS

MUZZLE

BACK

CHIN GROOVE

THROAT LATCH

SHOULDER

FLANK

ELBOW

FOREARM

BARREL

CHESTNUT

STIFLE

KNEE

CANNON

ERGOT

PASTERN

HEEL

HOOF

Horse colours

There are 14,000 horses in training in the UK and another 8,500 in Ireland so, not surprisingly, they come in a variety of colours. This, and any particular markings on its body, has to be recorded in the horse's passport. It is up to the breeder and on-duty vet to agree on what colour the horse should be designated. As in humans, particular hair colours are hereditary, but others will often appear unexpectedly.

Bay

More than 70% of Thoroughbreds are classed as 'bay'. They look more obviously brown or even black to the eye but, according to Weatherbys' guidelines, there must be 'a reasonably clearly defined line of colour change between the black lower part of the legs and the general tan/brown colour of the upper legs and body'. The mane and tail are black.

Chestnut

At around 20%, chestnut is the second most common colour. Coats can vary almost across the spectrum from a dark red to a yellowy flaxen, also on the mane and tail.

Grey

Grey horses have always been popular with casual punters and are very easy to spot, standing out even more as they make up only around 3% of the population. They can vary dramatically from black and steel hues through to almost pure white. These

▼ A bay horse

▼ A chestnut horse

▼ A grey horse

horses will not have been born this exact colour as the grey comes from a genetic mutation. The foals could have started off in many different shades but the dominant grey gene will fade the pigment in its colouration. As this gene is passed on, every grey horse will have had at least one grey parent. It has no effect on performance, as grey horses have won all the major races. It can, though, sometimes be harder to assess their fitness when looking at their coat.

Other colours

Brown horses, where all the coat, legs, mane and tail are the same colour, also make up about 3%. There are actually very few (less than 0.5%) of the very striking and technically black

▲ A roan horse

horses. Other colours are rarely seen in Thoroughbreds, but can appear very occasionally and cause interest amongst racegoers. Roan, a mixture of white, brown and chestnut hairs, which can cause an almost pinkish hue, is an approved colour. All-white, almost albino racehorses have appeared on the track, as have the patchy skewbalds usually confined to the world of ponies.

◤ White Japanese Thoroughbred

▼ A black horse

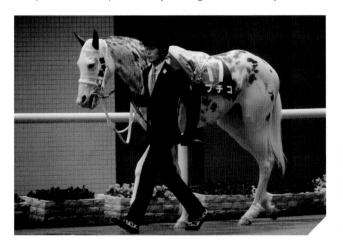

Horse identification

Thoroughbreds are all issued with a passport, not only so that they can be identified, but also to make sure that it is known who they belong to. These are kept at their stable, as they need to be taken with them when they go to the races. They contain a description of what the horse looks like, including certain markings, and their medical history, such as any vaccinations received, is entered in the back.

More recently horses in most racing nations have all had to be microchipped. This a small and largely painless procedure whereby a microchip is inserted into a ligament on the left side of the neck. It can be scanned quickly by a handheld device, similar to those used for finding the bargains in the supermarket.

The Flockton Grey conspiracy

Racing fiction authors have found rich pickings in the story of a 'ringer', in other words a horse that is not the one it is supposed to be. These do derive from true stories from the past, no more so than a notorious incident at Leicester racecourse back in 1982. A horse called Flockton Grey who had never run before, representing a small stable not renowned for having winners, galloped 20 lengths clear in a two-year-old race, landing a number of large bets.

Officials sounded the alarm and an investigator visited the Yorkshire stable of Stephen Wiles, concluding that Flockton Grey did not have the unusual scar on one leg, as was documented in his passport. Scrutiny of a few photographs

▼◢ The passport of Paul Nicholls' champion jumper Denman

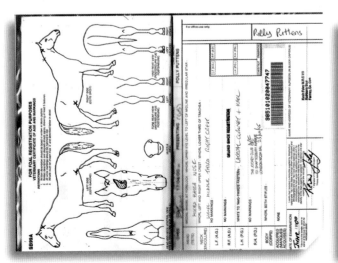

taken in the winners' enclosure concluded that the horse's teeth were also too developed to match those of a growing two-year-old. After trawling through thousands of records, it was discovered that the only other animal it could be was an older horse called Good Hand, who was eventually found months later in a field by reporters.

Ken Richardson, the owner of Flockton Grey, was eventually convicted of conspiracy to defraud, with a heavy fine and a suspended nine-month prison sentence. It is believed he organised the duping of an unsuspecting vet to give Good Hand a passport with the details of Flockton Grey, as well as the switching of the horses on the way to the races.

Markings

The number of markings that a horse can have on its body and head are virtually unlimited. They are recorded in the form of an accurate and annotated sketch on the passport.

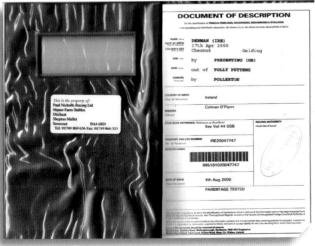

Everything must be recorded, including areas where the coat is flecked with different colours, and whorls, which are changes in direction of the growth of the hair. They commonly have white feet or legs, and sometimes they even have splashes of white around the stomach.

Those with particularly unusual markings tend to attract a cult following among the racing fraternity. Most horses have what is known as a 'chestnut', which is a small wart-like growth just above the knee. It looks a little unsightly and is believed to be a remnant of something that was needed by the horse's distant ancestors, but has evolved into a completely harmless accessory.

PROMINENT MARKINGS ON A HORSE'S HEAD

▲ A star on the forehead of top-class jumper, The New One

▼ A blaze
▶ An almost white face

Star	Any white mark on the forehead.
Stripe	A narrow white mark that runs down the bridge of the nose.
Blaze	A thicker white mark that covers almost the whole of the forehead between the eyes and extends through the width of the nose down to the muzzle.
White face	Where the forehead and the front of the face are covered by white.
Snip	A white mark between or around the nostrils.

Drug testing in horses

Partly in reaction to some high-profile cases involving the administration of anabolic steroids earlier this century, testing has become far tighter and global racing authorities are working hard towards harmonising the rules around the world.

Although they were sometimes used during times when a horse was not competing, and to aid recovery rather than performance, there is now a zero-tolerance approach to steroids. Horses are not to be administered them at any time in their lives, or they could be prevented from racing or training for at least a year, and their keepers will face the music.

From as soon as they are registered with Weatherbys, officials must be aware of the whereabouts of a horse at all times and it must always be available for testing by blood or urine. Hair sampling, which tends to highlight prohibited substances for longer, is also being introduced. Other forms that fall under the zero-tolerance practice include various hormones and the manipulation of blood and cellular and genetic material.

Horses do need to be given various treatments from time-to-time and they are permitted if recommended by a vet, usually with a stand-down period before the animal can run again. However, on race day the horse is allowed only feed and water. Many years ago, a horse ate a groom's Mars bar and was disqualified after winning a race as it tested positive for a stimulant.

Testing also takes place in the racecourse stables. Samples are taken from winners of important races as well as some random selections and sent off to an independent laboratory.

There will always be people trying to transgress the rules in sport and there have been other cases around the world involving the use of performance enhancers such as cobalt or high doses of sodium bicarbonate to reduce the build-up of lactic acid. However, there have been great movements to stamp it out and widespread reductions in the use of anti-inflammatories such as phenylbutazone (bute) and Lasix (an anti-bleeding medication) have increased confidence that all competitors are on a level playing field.

▼ Prohibited substances can be detected in racehorses via blood testing

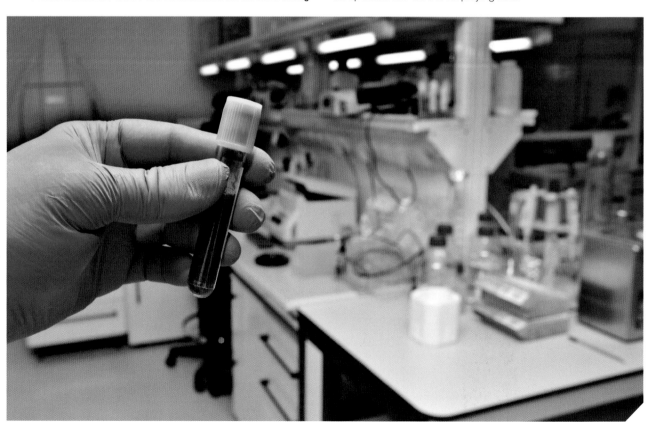

Performance issues

Just as with humans, horses are always picking up or getting over physical problems that require anything from a little bit of TLC and rest to extensive veterinary examinations, which in some cases may lead to career and life-threatening diagnoses. Sometimes there are obvious clues after a horse runs or exercises disappointingly and at other times nothing comes to light, even after exhaustive diagnostic examination.

Having regular access to an experienced vet is vital for a successful stable and in recent years, modern diagnostic techniques have improved the ability of vets to identify potential issues early on. For example, today a vet can even download an electrocardiogram application to their smart phone and most vets have access to portable digital diagnostic equipment, including radiography and ultrasound.

Some trainers like their horses to be blood tested on a monthly basis and samples are screened and analysed in a laboratory for any signs of health issues. This is usually repeated if a horse runs badly and the laboratory can report the results within an hour. Horses requiring more in-depth diagnostic investigations, treatment or surgery will be referred to a specialist equine hospital, which will have facilities similar to a human hospital, including operating theatres and an intensive care unit, only on a larger scale.

Thankfully, veterinary science and expertise has improved to the extent that these days, horses can recover from most injuries and there are many modern forms of treatment and surgical procedures available. For example, many surgical procedures today can now be carried out in the standing horse, using sedation and local anaesthetic, without the need for general anaesthesia.

Dentist

Tooth pain can be an issue. Some stables will bring a specialist equine dentist in to look at the horses a couple of times a year, but many good vets are also able to deal with problem teeth. Mainly the treatment will involve filing off rough edges, which can cause issues with eating, or cause pain when they have a bit in the mouth.

Naturally, horses would wear down their teeth by chewing coarse food, but the diet of hay and hard feeds can cause the development of these edges. It is not irregular for a horse to need a tooth to be extracted, which is more of a process, but generally they are more accepting of a visit by the dentist than most humans would be.

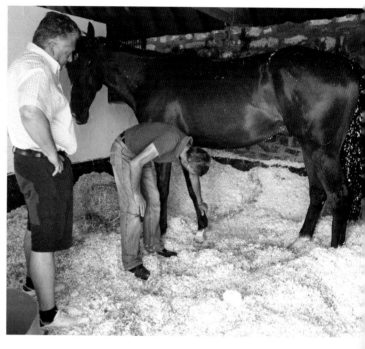

▲ Paul Nicholls and head lad Clifford Baker check a horse's legs as part of the daily routine

GELDING

As only the top-performing or best-bred colts will have a breeding career after racing, a decision usually has to be made early in their career as to whether an animal will be castrated or 'gelded'. Along with eliminating the chance of any unwanted new members of a stable, gelding has an important effect upon behaviour. Colts are easily distracted by fillies and can be bad-tempered and difficult to handle. Once gelded, they tend to settle down.

Gelding is carried out by a vet, under sedation and local anaesthetic, in some cases these days with the horse standing up. It is a swift process, involving incisions and a few cuts as the testicles are removed, but it is considered to be relatively painless afterwards. A horse often loses a little of its weight after gelding, but it does not affect athletic performance and it should be ready to race again within a few weeks.

▲ A racehorse fitted with overground endoscopy equipment, which uses telemetry to enable vets to view the horse's upper airway during normal exercise conditions from a handheld computer
(Rossdales)

Respiratory problems

A significant performance-limiting issue concerns respiratory health, and a number of factors can cause or contribute to this. These can range from bacterial or viral infections to allergies to types of pollen or spores that appear at certain times of year, and can compromise a horse's natural immune system. This can manifest itself with a cough or snotty nose, although some horses can cough after inhaling more harmless dust spores or grains of sand. Some horses can even be asthmatic.

Respiratory issues reduce the efficiency of the exchange between oxygen and carbon dioxide, resulting in muscles tiring more quickly. The margins can seem very small, yet make a huge difference in how a horse runs. Such problems are usually explored by performing an endoscopic examination – better known as a 'scope'. This involves inserting a flexible instrument with a small camera on its end through the horse's nostril to enable viewing of the horse's upper airway while it is at rest.

Some racehorse trainers are keen on scoping their horses very regularly – and particularly before a race – to make sure that the horse's airway is clear, while others are reluctant to do so at all. It is up to the trainer to trust their judgement, although if the horses are healthy and running well, there is probably no need to do so. Using this equipment, it is also possible to carry out a tracheal wash, where a saline solution is flushed into the windpipe and drawn back up with a syringe. This collected liquid can be sent off for laboratory analysis of the cells.

It will not always be an infection that is to blame for poor performance – some respiratory issues are derived from anatomical problems. Endoscopic examination can be carried out in the exercising horse using a technique called overground endoscopy, which allows the vet to identify any physical abnormalities in the upper airway that may affect the horse's performance. A horse can be found to be making a roaring or gurgling noise during exercise, which will usually indicate issues associated with the larynx, epiglottis or soft palate, and there are veterinary procedures commonly referred to as 'wind operations' that can help the horse to breathe correctly again.

During an overground endoscopy examination, the horse will be fitted with an endoscope and a small computer will be attached to the horse's saddle cloth, which then transmits data to a handheld device that shows live images of the horse's upper respiratory tract while the horse is being exercised. This method allows the vet to quickly and accurately determine any abnormalities in the horse's upper airway.

Injuries

Accidents can happen at the racecourse, the stable, or even when the horse is on its summer holidays. Lameness is a common issue in keeping a horse out of action and should be easy to identify, certainly to a well-trained eye, if the horse does not want to bear weight on a particular leg or foot. On other occasions, lameness will be more obvious to a rider due to the way the horse has been moving and responding to instruction.

The problem can be as simple as a bruised foot, perhaps caused by walking on a stone or due to having been kicked by another horse, which will usually resolve very quickly. Otherwise it could be because of athletic injuries such as a sprained joint, a sore knee, a pulled muscle or even a fracture. It is good practice for trainers or their staff to run their hands down a horse's legs daily, checking for any swelling or hot areas.

However, a horse has 205 bones in its body and they all need to be aligned and working in harmony in order for it to perform at its best. If the vet is unable to localise the problem easily, the horse may be referred to an equine hospital for further diagnostic tests, which may include nerve blocks, x-rays, MRI, CT or even a bone scan to discover precisely what is wrong. Bone scanning involves the injection of a radioactive isotope, which attaches to bone and will highlight 'hotspots' on the horse's skeleton when images are taken with a gamma ray camera. Inflammation, soft tissue and tendon damage can be seen as well as bone breaks. During this process, the horse becomes mildly radioactive and will have to go to an isolation stable for 24 hours.

It has become increasingly possible to carry out operations in the standing horse, using a combination of local anaesthetic and sedation, but in more complicated cases the horse will require general anaesthesia. During the recovery period following surgery, careful management of the horse is essential

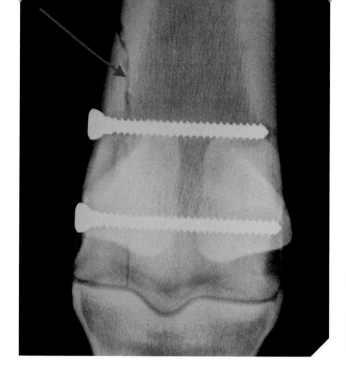

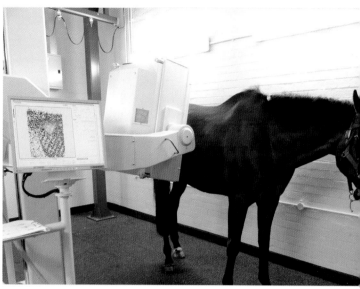

▲ Cannon bone (long bone) fractures occur mainly in young racehorses. This fracture (indicated by arrow) was amenable to surgical repair. Many fractures can now be repaired while the horse is standing, using local anaesthetic and sedation *(Rossdales)*

▲ Bone scanning uses radioactive tracers that attach to bone. When using a gamma camera, increases in bone turnover show up as 'hot spots'. This imaging technique is useful for detecting changes in bone metabolism before they become visible on x-rays – for example, hairline fractures *(Rossdales)*

to ensure that it doesn't re-injure itself. A calm temperament is a great help in these cases.

For soft tissue injuries, vets have a number of options available to them in aiding diagnosis and treatment, including a range of regenerative medicine treatments such as stem cell therapy. Trainers often employ equine physiotherapists who can work alongside their vet to treat various muscle and ligament injuries.

Colic and other problems

Even a few years ago, colic was considered a death sentence in racehorses. It can still be fatal but numbers have been dramatically reduced with a greater understanding of the problem. Colic is essentially abdominal pain, and can affect around 5% of horses at some point in their life, varying from extremely mild to severe. Typical signs are that a horse will lie down more often or get up and down frequently, or more dramatically, they can start pawing at the ground or kicking at their stomach.

Colic can be caused by a plethora of factors. It often derives from a change in a horse's diet, perhaps from ingesting something it shouldn't have, from changes in management and stabling, or it can be stress-related. The horse could also be dehydrated or suffering from excess gas.

An estimated 90% of cases will resolve themselves on their own, helped by plenty of fresh air and water, with no treatment needed. In the cases where the intestine has become twisted and is cutting off blood supply, or there is a foreign object present, surgery may be required. Providing veterinary treatment

is sought promptly, the majority of horses will be able to run again once they have recovered.

Horses are susceptible to many illnesses, from colds to pneumonia, irritations and even skin cancer. One physical issue found in many young racehorses is sore shins, which is an inflammation of the cannon bone, and related to bone immaturity when the horse's skeleton cannot cope with the additional strain it is placed under during training. This is usually resolved by reducing the work the horse is required to do for a period of time.

▲ Rossdales senior surgeon Richard Payne operates on a horse under general anaesthesia *(Rossdales)*

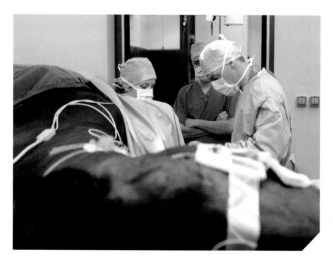

Famous horses

Arkle

Irish chaser Arkle is considered the greatest jumps horse of all time, not only on official ratings but also in the hearts of the public, and it is unlikely this status will ever be challenged. He not only won 27 races out of 35, but he also won the Cheltenham Gold Cup three times consecutively from 1964 to 1966.

What was perhaps most impressive was that Arkle would run in handicap races, carrying on at least one occasion as much as 2st more weight than his competitors. Running in handicaps on unfavourable terms is a task rarely attempted by the best modern jumpers, who keep to level-weight competition.

Trained by Tom Dreaper and running in the yellow and black colours of the Duchess of Westminster, Arkle is a folk hero in Ireland, often referred to only as 'Himself' and he features prominently in cultural history. When he suffered what was to be a career-ending injury at Kempton Park in 1966, he had to convalesce at the course for a few months and was sent reams of fan mail and get well cards.

Frankel

It is very unusual for a racehorse to remain unbeaten throughout their career, as nearly all have an off day or are unlucky in a race. There was never an off day for Frankel, who won all of his 14 starts in Britain between 2010 and 2012. The colt had the breeding to make a star, as his father was the champion stallion Galileo and the esteemed Sir Henry Cecil trained him. He was named after another great trainer, the late American Bobby Frankel, and showed promise from the outset. Frankel's most memorable performance was in the 2000 Guineas at Newmarket in 2011 when, instead of being settled conventionally in the pack, he tore off in the lead and was never close to being caught. Frankel's stride length was measured to be a foot longer than the average horse and he used it to dismantle every new rival sent to defeat him. He was retired to become a stallion in 2012 and topped the all-time Flat ratings by all the respected authorities.

▼ Frankel is the highest-ranked horse since modern ratings began

Sprinter Sacre was given the nickname 'The Black Aeroplane' after his towering performances

Seabiscuit

A hero of the Great Depression, Seabiscuit's achievements were so considerable that a Hollywood feature film was made about him in 2003. He was an ordinarily bred small horse who was difficult to train in his early days and fairly hopeless on the track, winning only a few from an arduous campaign at two and three years old. It was not until he was bought and moved to a new trainer, Tom Smith, that his career took off. The unconventional cowboy, Smith found the secret to him and he built up a partnership with jockey John 'Red' Pollard, winning important races across the country in the mid-1930s. Both Seabiscuit and Pollard, who kept it secret that he was blind in one eye, were to suffer serious injuries, but came together for a stunning swansong when winning the 1940 Santa Anita Handicap.

Sprinter Sacre

The greatest jumper of the post-Arkle era was born and bred in France and bought as part of a job lot of 22 by owners Raymond and Caroline Mould. Sprinter Sacre was sent to trainer Nicky Henderson in Lambourn and marked out as well above average in bumper and hurdle races.

It was when he was moved up to steeplechase fences in 2011 that this beautiful black-coated specimen began to look exceptional, embarking upon a ten-race winning streak in two-mile races, which included an emphatic win in the Queen Mother Champion Chase at Cheltenham. Sprinter Sacre then suffered from an irregular heartbeat in a race at Kempton, which kept him off the track for more than a year, and it was only into the 2015–16 season that he rediscovered his form, culminating in a memorable performance when he regained the Champion Chase.

Red Rum

No British horse has ever really had a following like Red Rum, whose record in the Grand National of three wins (1973, 1974, 1977) and seconds in the intervening years will probably never be surpassed. Part of Red Rum's identity stemmed from his charismatic trainer Ginger McCain, who prepared the horse from an unprepossessing stable behind a car showroom in Southport near Liverpool.

Red Rum was by far at his best when running at his local track and seemed to love the challenge of the big National fences, hunting down the clear lead established by Crisp in his first big win and raising the roof on his final one. The horse was retired through injury before the 1978 National and went on to tour the country as an equine celebrity.

Phar Lap

Bred in New Zealand and trained in Australia, the horse fondly nicknamed 'Big Red' was the wonder of the southern hemisphere. Phar Lap accumulated a phenomenal winning streak and had already reached such a high profile prior to his victory in the Melbourne Cup in 1930 that for some reason gunmen attempted to shoot him (luckily they missed) after his final preparatory track work exercise.

He continued to dominate the Australian scene before an intrepid decision was made, against the wishes of trainer Harry Telford, to ship him to Mexico in 1932 for an incredibly valuable race called the Agua Caliente Handicap, which he also won. He died not long after in America, when found in pain by his groom, and theories have long abounded that Phar Lap was poisoned. His stuffed hide is displayed in the Melbourne Museum.

The stable

The stables are where the horse will spend most of its working life. They can range hugely from old-fashioned brick and wooden blocks to light and airy state-of-the-art barns. Stables have traditionally been based close to the main racecourses for ease of access, but there are others spread across the countryside of many European nations. They vary significantly depending upon their ownership; some are private enterprises with all of their own facilities, whilst others share and use quite public areas for exercising the horses. In much of America and Asia, horses are mostly housed in blocks adjoining or very near to the racecourse itself.

The trainer

Preparing the horse to run in races is the responsibility of the trainer. In the case of those running large stables, though, the role is more comparable to being the chief executive of a business, with many equine and human workers under their control. A trainer of five horses might do everything themselves – from mucking out and riding them to all of the administration. However, it is not unusual for a trainer to have 200 horses, and in this case they are never going to have time to oversee the interests of each.

Each horse must have a plan made for it and have its progress monitored. When it is ready, the trainer must start looking through the programme of races scheduled for the year and finding suitable ones. The horse will be entered for a race or races a week in advance and the trainer will study the weather forecast, possible rivals and available jockeys to assess whether it looks a suitable opportunity. If it is, the horse will be confirmed (or declared) to run a day or two before.

At the time of the race, the trainer is responsible for saddling the horse correctly, meeting the owner and discussing the tactics with the jockey.

There are always new horses to bring in and others that need to be moved on, as well as the physical jobs of maintaining the facilities and machinery that keep the show going. Delegation is necessary and the leading operations will have a pyramid of assistants, secretaries, work riders and stable staff.

A trainer wants to keep their horses and to get more sent to them in the future, so it is important to keep their owners happy. This can be achieved by a simple phone call or email every week informing them of the horse's progress and when it might next run. The more demanding might necessitate attending a few lunches and dinners and plenty of schmoozing and special treatment. Racing is a competitive world and there is always someone with an empty stable ready to take in a new horse.

Becoming a trainer

The job of a trainer has long appeared an aspirational one, with golden mornings spent watching gleaming Thoroughbreds and afternoons spent winning races. For a few at the top end of society, it is something of a rite of passage. It is, of course, mostly far less glamorous and will take time, determination and discipline to get in to.

▶ Trainer Paul Nicholls

Cost is the biggest factor and a prospective trainer needs to find a base – either to rent or buy – and work out if it is feasible, as well as becoming qualified to get started. Candidates will have already been working at a stable for five years, with at least two in a senior capacity, before they are considered for the mandatory training courses and, ultimately, applying to the BHA for a licence.

First of all, a 'level three' diploma in horse care and management is required. These are in the form of one- or two-year courses offered at many colleges, much of which is work-based assessment and mainly involves knowing how to look after horses properly. Then the trainer must attend three different short courses of around a week at the British Racing School in Newmarket.

Only then is it possible to go through the BHA's licensing procedure. The application is strict and involves the provision of a business plan, character references, correct insurance,

and proof that they have at least three horses ready for training and have access to at least £40,000 available in capital or as an overdraft. Facilities and backgrounds will be checked and applicants must demonstrate that they are capable of beginning training and employing staff, as well as understanding everything they are required to do.

Staff

Working in a racing stable is not a way to earn your fortune or for those who enjoy lie-ins. The pay is low, staff will be lucky to get one weekend off in two and it has been hard for many to recruit enough suitable candidates. On the flip side, it is a job of great camaraderie, being outdoors and dealing with magnificent animals on a daily basis. Having reliable staff to ensure the horses are receiving the best possible care is vital. A trainer is reliant on their feedback and the very best staff are at a premium.

The assistant trainer

Depending on the size of the stable, a trainer will usually need a right-hand person. To begin with, a more junior 'pupil' assistant usually shadows the trainer everywhere, possibly driving them to the races and slowly learning the ropes.

As they progress, this can lead to having the responsibility of looking after a whole barn and making sure the horses are healthy and out for exercise at the right time. They can be put in charge of a sub-team, which is something less for the trainer to worry about and prepares the assistant for a time when they might want to branch out on their own. They might represent the trainer at the races if the stable has runners at different meetings and will be in constant contact with the boss.

▼ Working with valuable horses is one of the highlights of employment in a racing stable

▼ Paul Nicholls' long-serving head lad Clifford Baker riding stable superstar Kauto Star on the gallops

The head lad/lass

This is the trainer's person on the ground, who will be married to the yard, getting there first in the morning (perhaps as early as 5am) and being the last out at night. The head lad or lass is likely to have progressed up the ladder and will know every horse inside out, usually organising the first feeding themselves. It is their job to make sure the rest of the staff arrive on time and know what they are doing.

Many stables have their own staff accommodation, much like a hostel, and this can be the first time a new young employee has ever lived away from home. Nowadays, the realities of staff shortages means that many workers arrive from overseas and need somewhere to live, at least temporarily. The rest of the staff is usually recruited locally and someone will always be on-site or on-call in case of an emergency.

Grooms/lads and lasses

The rest of the staff will usually arrive a little after the head lad or lass and will have around four horses each to look after. The first job in the morning is to muck out each horse by removing and replacing any soiled or damp bedding before putting on the tack so they are ready for exercise. Most trainers send their horses out in three groups or 'lots', so some will come back in and be washed down, then the next group will be readied for their work, with a short break for breakfast in between.

Most staff will also ride, but part-time riders and fully fledged jockeys will also come in to help out. Full-timers have a break from lunchtime until mid-afternoon, skip out (remove any more droppings) and then spend perhaps 20 minutes grooming each of their horses. Coats are combed, brushed and sometimes clipped in order for the horse to look more presentable.

▲ There is plenty of camaraderie between staff through early starts and long days

Before races, manes can be plaited and shapes brushed onto the hindquarters as there are often cash prizes for the staff responsible for the 'best turned out' in the paddock. Hooves are oiled, feet are thoroughly cleaned and rugs are put on to ensure the animals do not get cold at night.

In spending every day with a horse, often for many years, staff can become very attached to them and might have favourite characters that they might prefer to lavish more time and attention on. There will be a hierarchy at larger operations, involving assistants and travelling head grooms that oversee taking horses to the races, but the horse's usual groom will also accompany them to the track.

▼ Mucking out is a necessary evil

▼ A student with the Northern Racing College keeps their charge looking smart

Teaching a horse to race

A horse will usually be sent to a trainer a few months before it is ready to run. For young two-year-olds that are just starting out, it will be a case of the trainer assessing their level and finding out what they have got to work with, even if they have been pre-trained somewhere else. It all boils down to taking everything slowly and ensuring that they become more responsive to instructions from the rider. As with children at school, some will pick it up almost straight away and can be promoted to the top of the class, while others will require more intensive tutoring.

For the first couple of weeks, they might have a few sessions on a mechanical horse walker and be trotted around a field or paddock, just in case they are flighty or badly behaved. When they are ready, they can progress for a few weeks of longer walks and trotting around paths and lanes. This exercise will build up their conditioning and make fragile legs harder and stronger.

From here, they can start cantering. Very inexperienced horses will go out in groups in a quiet area without distractions and their riders will ask them to quicken up for a couple of furlongs. Those first steps are an unrestricted free-for-all, but once ready to train on the grown-up gallops the horses will usually be made to canter on their own, one behind another, before exercise becomes more organised. In order for them not to be fazed when surrounded by others in a race, they will start to canter alongside another, known in the trade as 'upsides', and become able to follow the pace set by a 'lead horse', which is usually a sensible older member of the stable.

Unless an owner wants the horse to be absolutely raring to go for its debut, the trainer would rather the learning process is gradual and the horse just enjoys its first experience on the track. It will probably only be given a push and asked to extend into a gallop for a short while on a couple of occasions before it races. The whip is rarely introduced in exercise, and often not in a first race if possible, as that is something the horse will become more accustomed to as it matures.

Knowing when a horse is ready for a race is often down to eye and instinct, but some trainers have become increasingly interested in technology such as heart monitors and GPS trackers, which help them to know how well a horse is exercising and recovering.

▼ Regular cantering builds up strength and endurance

▲ Roadwork strengthens horses up for the time they are ready to go on the gallops

GAITS

Movement in racing is described by four different gaits or running actions:

Walking
The slowest of movements, when the horse moves all of its legs on their own in a set order, with two or three on the ground at any time. A jockey can sit comfortably in the saddle.

Trotting
A quicker movement, more like jogging for humans, when the horse moves its legs in two sets of diagonal pairs at the same time and the jockey will have to move in time with the rhythm.

Cantering
When the horse breaks into a controlled run, where one leg supports the horse as the others move forward. The jockey will have to sit out of the saddle and will hear three rapid beats as hooves hit the ground.

Galloping
The fully fledged sprint mostly preserved for races, when all four legs strike the ground in quick succession, with a brief moment when all the legs are bent and off the ground.

▼ Horses move their legs in diagonals when trotting

Daily regime

Even a horse that has raced before but has been on a break will take two or three months to get fully fit, and although some may need some special treatment, it is easier in terms of staff and time management if they can join the programme of the majority of mature horses in the stable.

Trainers obviously have individual routines, but they tend to follow a similar pattern of being ridden five or six mornings a week. On Mondays, Tuesdays, Thursdays and Fridays, the horses will go for a regular canter along the gallops for a few furlongs to build up their fitness, while they might be asked to

▲ Horses, such as these trained by top British jumps trainer Nicky Henderson, become used to going out in large groups

pick up the pace and open up their lungs on what are known as 'work mornings' on a Wednesday or a Saturday.

If it is not their day to work, they might have a 40-minute session on the horse walker instead. Sundays, for humans and horses, are a day off; however, they still need to be entertained in some way. Usually they will be taken out for a walk in the morning, or turned out in a field to stretch their legs and socialise.

Once a horse is racing fit and running, most will retain their condition by simply continuing the process of cantering and

▼ The trainer's expert helper oversees morning exercise

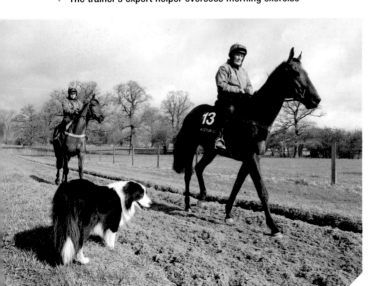

CALMING COMPANIONS

Some horses can be calmed down by being given a companion. As it is not practical or sometimes sensible for it to be another horse, a different friend is chosen. Sometimes it is a pony; American Pharoah, the brilliant US champion, would travel everywhere with Smokey the pony, and Seabiscuit had Pumpkin for company. Quite often goats are used and will go in the stable with the horses, while the stable cat and even pigs and chickens provide soothing company. Allez-France, a brilliant French-trained mare from the 1970s, would only live with a sheep and, when she was due to run abroad, a replacement had to be sought after her buddy ran into problems with US immigration.

walking. But a couple of weeks before an important race, a trainer might decide it needs to be reacquainted with the racecourse environment and take it by lorry to a track, where it will have a gallop.

When a horse is based in a big training centre or stabled near or next to a racecourse, it should be accustomed to the busy and distracting environment from an early age. On a racetrack, morning exercise routines are carried out in public and punters and enthusiasts can get acquainted with them. Many countries even publish times of each horse's exercises.

Those trained in private areas will not have encountered many other horses before their first race, and their potential ability is only likely to be known by those with a connection to the stable.

The gallops

Morning exercises for most horses take place on the gallops, which can differ enormously depending on location and the way in which the trainer wants to build up the strength and fitness of their horses.

In times gone by, work would always be carried out on grass and those on the chalkier and freer-draining lands would fare best during the worst of the weather. It was only at the beginning of the 20th century that grounds workers in racing's heartland of Newmarket began to add layers of peat moss to some areas, in order to create a springy surface that would be safe for use by horses when other places had become too firm. The tradition has continued ever since.

▲ Some of the top stables have a number of different gallops, such as these at Philip Hobbs' base near Minehead in Somerset

By the 1970s, this had been overtaken by a need to provide something that would be usable on a year-round basis, and was less susceptible to the elements. Strips began to be laid with woodchips and fibres, or sand. There are many of these still in use today, as they are reliable and kind on the limbs. As a horse is most likely to be racing on grass, it can be useful to let it have a practice spin on it when conditions allow.

▼ A horse is washed down after morning exercise

Providing gallops surfaces is a lucrative business – it costs a hefty sum to cover half a mile of ground with a suitable depth of material. Technology has moved on with many newer gallops fitted with various substances similar to those found on all-weather racecourses, usually a wax-coated combination of silica, artificial fibres and recycled material. They are intended to last for many years before they have to be replaced. The way in which they are laid out depends on the available topography and the ideas of the trainer. Some prefer to boost endurance to the maximum by getting the horses to make their way up a steep hill. Others have smaller, flatter loops to work with and get the blood pumping with sessions through deep sand.

The variety of facilities that can be seen from successful trainers in every corner prove that there is no blueprint to getting it right.

Routine at Paul Nicholls' stable

Jump horses will generally require longer, steadier exercises to get them fit, as the trainer Paul Nicholls explains:

My philosophy is to work the horses hard to get them fit, and work them hard to keep them fit. Most will do two hours a day, which would entail an hour on the walker and an hour or an hour and a quarter being ridden.

▼ The horse walker is an integral part of the Paul Nicholls training regime

We keep it simple. We have a variation of facilities with a steep hill, which is five furlongs, another flat five-furlong gallop and two oval tracks of 400m. We try to use a combination of them, and horses might do two or three canters up the hill or mix it up with the flat gallop. It's all interval training and not a huge mileage, but involves lots and lots of hard graft.

Sometimes they will canter on the 400m round track, eight circuits each way, and then go on the flat track. The hill is like going up the side of Mount Everest, so they are certainly doing their bit. I've always been an advocate of not doing the actual galloping at home and leaving that for the racecourse.

We are very big on schooling and they will usually do this once a week. We put four jumps on one of the 400m tracks – they will do four circuits each way so they are probably jumping 32 times.

The two mechanical horse walkers are on the go from six in the morning to six at night. We never stop using them, and some of the heavier, lumpier types might even have two hours on the walker as well as an exercise on the gallops; some others might have a day off riding and just have an hour on the walker instead. Their only day off is Sunday, but if they are running on a Monday they might possibly still go out for one canter. If they are due to run the following week, they might have an hour on the walker just to keep them ticking along.

Horses that are not running on through the summer will have from the middle of May until the middle of July off and just go out in the field, weather permitting.

Most health issues are resolved by having a good routine.

Every summer the stables will be completely emptied for 28 days, steam-cleaned and disinfected. That's a golden rule to hopefully kill any bugs and make it all healthy.

You've just got to be careful and use common sense. A sick horse must be immediately put in quarantine and ones that come in from other yards and the sales will not be introduced to the main environment until we're sure everything's OK.

Ideally they will have eight weeks out at grass during a 12-month period and it will take 12 weeks minimum to get one ready to win. Some might get away with 10, some might want more.

Health and fitness is the key to it all. You soon get to know that some will need a run to be at their best. I like to think that the art is to have them fit enough to win first time out, but be fit enough to improve. It doesn't always work like that, but you've got a fair idea when they are ready to run just by knowing the amount of graft that they've done, the way they look, and their recovery rate after working. A lot will fly up our hill and have a real good blow afterwards; it might even take 20 minutes before they stop. Others will stop blowing almost instantly and you know that they are fit.

My head lad and I have to rely on what we think. Sometimes you will get one of the lads saying that he's not going very well, but we might just know that he's a slow horse. You've got to follow your own feeling a bit. You must listen to what they say but it's not exclusive. You're putting everything together and trying to make a plan.

▲ Horses at Paul Nicholls' stable undertake hearty exercise on the steep uphill gallop

▼ Paul Nicholls oversees a schooling session

Feeding

Just as footballers no longer enjoy steak and chips and a couple of cigarettes before going out on the field, neither do elite racehorses get given just Guinness, oats and the odd apple. Horse feeding has become far more sophisticated, and as most stables do not have the time to combine their own recipes of grains, they buy them pre-prepared from leading suppliers, such as British firm Baileys or Ireland's Red Mills.

In order for the fussy types not to start picking their favourite bits out, many trainers opt for a dry cubed form of food, made from blended oats, soya, alfalfa, wheat and linseed, bound together with various oils and often with added vitamins and minerals. Theoretically, this provides horses with the right amount of protein, carbohydrate and fat to help with growth and energy supply. Horses have a sweet tooth and feeds are usually flavoured with sugar beet molasses in order to make them more palatable. The odd treat by way of a carrot or a peppermint is not prohibited.

Those that dislike the cubes can be given a loose form of the feed, while the main companies make a huge range of different products, varying from those for young horses to those with specific dietary requirements. A racehorse eats a lot – they are usually fed first thing at about 6am, then at lunchtime and finally in the early evening, and get through eight to ten kilograms of

▲ A busy stable will get through a lot of food!

food per day. Considering a bag might cost £15 for 20kg, it is easy to see why they start costing so much.

A clue to the health of a horse is whether it is eating well and the little-and-often technique is a similar mantra applied by human athletes. It is said that one leading trainer even has a

▼ Horses can consume bucketloads of hay

▲ Water buckets must be topped-up to keep horses hydrated
(British Racing School)

▲ Brushes and brooms are in regular use to keep the stable clean

staff member employed to offer more food at midnight should any of the residents still be peckish. Rivals are always interested in what each other are giving their horses, should there be any way of gaining that little extra advantage.

Hay

In the natural world, a horse would spend all day grazing on grasses. In order to replicate this herbivorous lifestyle they are given abundant quantities of dry hay, usually coarser varieties of rye and meadow grass. Plenty is grown domestically but latterly some establishments have been espousing the benefits of expensive imported Canadian hay.

Hay has a number of uses for a horse. It not only provides a level of vitamins, but its fibre and roughage are vital for the digestive system. It keeps the gut working, converting fibre into energy, and the act of chewing creates saliva, which can reduce acidity in the stomach and prevent the development of problems such as ulcers.

It is important that there is always a ready supply of hay in the stable, and the horse will usually get through even more weight in hay than it does in food through the day. It has the further bonus of giving the animals something to do, particularly at night, as they tend not to sleep for more than four or five hours. Batches of hay arrive by the lorry load and possible contamination can be a major reason why viruses can be spread.

Racehorses thrive on routine and dislike change, but boredom can still be a problem in some. It is important to make sure this does not lead to the development of bad habits such as crib-biting, windsucking or pacing the stable. There is bustling activity and plenty of attention in the morning but it dies down after lunch when they are left to relax until the staff reappear in the early evening. They are then left to themselves at night. Horses are easily enough pleased and activities that help to keep them occupied are being given a block of salt to lick, hanging a ball or rope in the stable or just playing the radio.

Just as horses eat, so too do they drink. The horse's system is powered by a huge amount of water and, depending on the weather and the amount of activity it has had, a horse might get through 40 litres of it every day. Buckets and troughs must be replenished, while some modern stables have even invested in automatic refilling systems.

The kit

Headgear

From an aesthetic point of view, horses look much better just wearing an ordinary bridle. It should also signal that they are straightforward to ride and, theoretically, will give their supporters an honest run for their money. When trainers feel that their horse is capable of offering more than they have been doing so far, they can look for some form of assistance. Most have to be declared on the racecard and the fitting of some types of headgear, particularly for the first time, can be a good pointer if it works and brings about an improved performance.

Cheekpieces

Also known in different jurisdictions as French blinkers or winkers, these are a roll of sheepskin that attaches by Velcro to the side of the bridle. They are considered the gentlest way of providing some help to a horse that isn't concentrating on racing ahead, as they stop them from

▼ An assortment of different headgear can be used to get the best out of a horse

looking behind but still offer peripheral vision and a good view of the horse's environment.

Blinkers

A more extreme option for horses comes in the way of a hood that goes under the bridle, with a half-open cup around the eyes. The idea is to create tunnel vision, cutting out any sideways view. Most horses wearing blinkers are considered difficult and unreliable, but they can be used simply to provide more confidence to a horse that can feel a little intimidated by its surroundings and they can also act like a comfort blanket. A visor is almost identical, but has a small slit cut into the blinker to allow light and a sense of other horses around.

Noseband

A strip of sheepskin that attaches to the loop of the bridle that goes around the nose. They are usually used if a horse carries its head a bit high and becomes less focussed and more difficult to ride, although some trainers use them out of habit. As horses look down their nose when they are going forward, it obstructs the view and makes them drop their head to look over it.

▲ Cheekpieces

▲ Blinkers

▲ Sheepskin noseband

▲ A hood

Other pieces of headgear

A hood is like the blinkers but without the vision restrictive cups and covers the ears, muffling sound to help a sensitive horse. Similarly, earplugs can be inserted to drown out any outside noise. An eyeshield, which has a mesh surrounding the eyes of a hood, allows some light in and can also prevent any flying material getting in the eyes. A strip of material called a tongue-tie can aid both breathing and safety for a horse.

Bridles and saddles

It will always be an unequal battle between small jockey and big horse, so the bridle allows the rider to try to remain in control. On the whole, stables try to keep the steering equipment as simple as possible. This would usually be a 'cavesson' noseband, a simple strap that goes around the nose and below the jaw that keeps the mouth closed and stops the horse trying to avoid keeping the bit in. This will be combined with a ring bit (usually called a loose ring snaffle), which goes in the mouth and attaches to the reins.

▼ A stable tack room houses a huge amount of equipment

▲ **Tacking up takes quite a bit of practice** *(Northern Racing College)*

There are numerous variations that can be used. If a horse pulls very hard and keeps opening its mouth and crossing its jaw, making it harder to control, it can wear a more severe-looking crossed, or grackle, noseband. This was famously worn by the great Frankel. An Australian noseband, which is often in orange rubber, is another common sight. It runs up the middle of the forehead and keeps the bit up towards the roof of the horse's mouth, discouraging the horse from trying to get its tongue over the top of the bit. The bit itself can vary in accordance with the size of the horse's mouth and how they behave, while some will not have a noseband, and instead will have a ring running around the bottom of the jaw. A martingale,

a leather strap that attaches to the girth underneath a horse and can be fixed underneath the noseband, is often used on horses at the stable, but not at the races. This stops a horse from carrying its head too high.

At the stables, many of those who exercise horses are bigger than the race-day jockeys and there is a greater need for comfort for both horse and rider, so horses will usually have larger saddles, a saddle pad and towel or chamois to prevent it slipping, and a large saddlecloth.

Shoes

With a few exceptions, all racehorses wear shoes from the time they are first sent to a sales or stable. It prevents the hoof from wearing down while the horse is out and about, as well as protecting from potential environmental infections. The hoof is always growing, so when the farrier comes to fit a new pair of shoes, they will clean out and file the hoof down before hammering the shoe into the perfect shape and fitting it. During its training routine, which will often involve being on roads, the horse is likely to need a new set every three weeks. Regular shoes are made from a lightweight, hardwearing steel, but several days before a race these will be replaced by even lighter aluminium racing shoes.

There are a number of different types of remedial shoes for horses that have feet problems. Around 5% are unsuited to having shoes that are hammered into place with small nails, so they have a stick-on version instead. Becoming a farrier is a dangerous job, given so much time is spent being up close to such temperamental animals. It not only requires an academic qualification, but also the serving of a long apprenticeship.

▼ **Lightweight shoes, made of aluminium, are fitted close to a race**

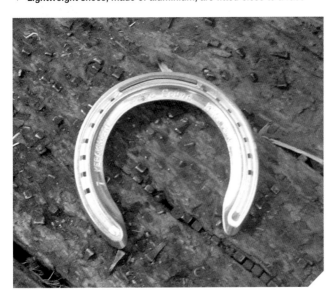

▼ **It takes a long time to learn the skills to become a farrier** *(www.godolphin.com)*

Race practice and schooling

▲ A set of practice stalls at the Northern Racing College

'If they don't jump, they don't win,' said one famous jumps trainer from the past, and 'schooling' practice is vital for a jump horse. Some horses will have been taught how to jump from an early age. Even if they are running in bumper races for their first season, they still need to start gentle schooling, usually with a rider, but occasionally they can be carefully encouraged to jump loose.

Many will be naturals at it and take to the discipline immediately. In some cases, though, this will be a laborious process over many months, trying to get horses to pick their feet up over very small showjumping poles and plastic barrels before they can start moving on to replica hurdles and fences. Schooling keeps a horse's eye in and stretches the muscles, as well as helping with fitness. It will also aid them when they are running and build confidence. As much as they might be happy flying over fences when full of energy, they need to still be able

to do it when they are tiring. Schooling is of similar benefit to jockeys, as you cannot ride over too many obstacles.

For a Flat racer, one of the fundamental skills to pick up is jumping out of the stalls, but this will not require as intensive sessions. They might have been led into a small replica set of starting gates as a yearling and allowed to stand there for a minute or so to become used to the confinement. Those that are sensitive to being touched around the sides or legs will make it perfectly obvious, and can then wear a rug the next time they try it. A month or so before the horse is ready to race, it will have some further tuition where the stalls can be opened up and closed in front and behind them in order for them to get used to the idea. It should be allowed to leave the stalls

▲ Schooling helps a horse to jump accurately when it comes to a race

because it wants to, rather than because of being pushed or frightened. There are a few specialists at equine behaviour that can be brought in if the horse is difficult at this stage.

Barrier trials and schooling races

Most of what needs to be done with a horse will be within its comfort zone at home, but not everything can be replicated, especially if a trainer is based on his or her own, out in the countryside. Sometimes, they need a push.

In some jurisdictions 'barrier trials' are mandatory and they are important pieces of preparation in countries such as Hong Kong and Australia, where each one is video recorded. In France, there are races confined to young jockeys learning at the racing school and no betting is permitted. In most cases, they are for two- or three-year-old horses that have not raced before, and it is more about the learning process than pure fitness, but not always.

Barrier trials are basically practice races where the horse will have the experience of going in a lorry to the races, being saddled in the racecourse stable, walking around the paddock and getting to the track. Runners are loaded into the stalls and set out for a race over a few furlongs – the only difference being that there are no rules about having to try to win and they do not count as an official run in the records. Depending on how important the exercise is regarded by their owner and trainer, the horse can either be ridden harder or allowed to coast around in its own time.

In Ireland, and to a far lesser extent in Britain, there are schooling races where a large group of runners will jump a few hurdles in heats over around two miles. The schooling days at many of the significant Irish racecourses are open to the public, but it is not exactly a spectator-friendly experience. There is no commentary or ready publication of the names that are involved. In the build-up to the Cheltenham Festival each March, it is not unusual for even quite well-known horses to appear in a schooling race to sharpen them up for the big day.

◀ Horses can tune up for a race with a racecourse gallop
(Keeneland Photo)

However, many trainers would rather keep it quiet in case their headline horse performs badly, or even so well that it alerts the interest of bookmakers.

Other training aids

As with any type of athlete, horses are not always in the shape to be racing or in full training and some stables have a number of machines that aid with injury or act as a step before they get back into their routine. Some are extremely expensive and beyond the means of most stables to have themselves, but there are plenty of equine facilities that offer them for one-off or regular use.

Swimming pool

Horses, some might be surprised to learn, are able to swim. It comes naturally to them, although some enjoy it more than others, and it is a gentle process to get them accustomed to the strange surroundings of an equine swimming pool. An equine pool does not look hugely different to a normal pool, only they are usually in a ring shape with a platform in the middle where an assistant will stand. Using a single rein – or often one either side to keep hold, steer and make sure the horse does not get its head under the water – it can then do laps around the pool.

Swimming is generally used as part of the recovery process after a horse has been injured, rather than a regular part of the routine. This resistance training will build up muscle and improve the horse's fitness, without the danger of putting pressure on a tender back or legs or causing any further problems.

A common strategy is to swim in short intervals, with perhaps a couple of minutes of swimming and then a couple of minutes resting. It is fairly intensive work and a horse will not need too many sessions before it starts to make a difference. Irish trainer Robbie McNamara, very much an advocate of using swimming in his schedule, believes there have been a few horses in his care that would not have been sound enough to return to racing without using the pool.

▼ **Swimming lessons are always closely monitored**
(www.godolphin.com)

◀ A horse casts a long reflection in the swimming pool

While it is mostly used for this purpose, it is sometimes used to give a change of routine to a horse that has seemed to be stuck in a rut, and also acts as a quick cooling-down session.

Water walker

Similar to the standard horse walker, only with water that can be filled up to the waist or shoulder, a water walker has become a more popular technique in recent years. It is generally used as an addition to standard exercise and a horse can be put into them on its own for about 40 minutes.

There is also a water treadmill, which looks like a large bathtub with a moving floor and can either be used to help horses that are slowly coming back to fitness or for horses that are already there.

▶ The water walker is a helpful addition to the daily exercise regime (www.godolphin.com)

▼ An equine spa has become a modern way of easing aches and pains in a horse (ECB Equine)

◀ Horses can be slowly brought back to fitness using a state-of-the-art water treadmill *(ECB Equine)*

Horses mostly walk in these, but the settings can be quickened up, even to a canter. The principle of being both gentler and more effective than simply walking is the same in both. Horses will have less stress on their front legs and will start to use their back legs more to drive through the water. They are good for building up muscle towards the back and the powerful hindquarters.

Equine spas

Cold therapy is a big part of dealing with issues in horses' valuable but fragile legs. As one might take a bag of peas out of the freezer to relieve a bang on the head, an equine spa is invaluable if a trainer is worried that a horse has had a knock or is going to be sore or swollen.

An equine spa looks rather like standing a horse in the bath, but a little more space age, where the temperature of the salt water is between 2 and 4 degrees Celcius. It helps to improve circulation and oxygenation, to heal wounds and ease pain. The horse must not be allowed to get too cold, though, and they are not put in a spa for more than 15 minutes at a time. The use of salt water with horses is hardly a new one – part of three-time Grand National winner Red Rum's build-up was a dip on the beach, and visits to the sea are often part of the adventures organised by trainers from Ireland to South Africa and Australia if they are based near the coast. These equine spas have been steadily making their way into nearly all of the powerhouse racing stables.

Vibrating floors

Much like the power plate so beloved by the gym-goer, vibrations are believed to help horses work out. A platform fitted to a stable floor, covered with rubber and often able to tilt slightly, this machine allows horses to perform reflex actions with different muscle groups. It is supposed to improve circulation, increase bone and hoof growth and burn fat, helping with either rehabilitation or a training regimes.

Heat lamps

We all feel better with a bit of sun on our backs and it is no different for horses. Many trainers now have an area fitted with low-level, heat-producing infrared lamps. They are thought to cure all number of ills, but are particularly good for producing healthier skin and muscles. Horses usually like them too, and a session helps them to relax and feel better.

◀ Heat lamps

Transport

Every stable has a horsebox or two, depending on its size. For smaller operations, a lorry that can take a couple of horses in it will suit demands. However, those that might have a lot of runners at one meeting could have a 20-tonne juggernaut, complete with facilities for even the staff to have an overnight stay. Horses will usually have been used to travelling in a horsebox, either when being moved around as a foal or from being taken to a sale. There can be shows of reluctance to be led into the lorry from some, but others enjoy the change of the travelling experience. Legs will be bandaged and sometimes the boots will be put over the foot to protect them from either injuring themselves or getting moved around in the lorry.

In recent decades, the growing internationalisation of racing means horses will compete in other countries. Between Britain, Ireland and France, the usual and cheaper method is to simply take the horsebox on a ferry, but visits between Europe and America and the southern hemisphere mean air travel.

There are a few specialist transport companies that organise this complicated process, using either special charters or scheduled flights. The horses are loaded into a cargo aeroplane in converted crates with individual stables inside, usually two alongside each other so they have some company. They have shavings in their stable, hay and access to water, and once inside the plane they have access to their groom and are monitored by vets.

Some now even travel in compression suits designed to improve circulation and reduce muscle fatigue. Luckily, the horses do not seem to mind being dressed like an Olympic

▲ **A horse can spend time in quarantine when travelling internationally to prevent possible spreading of disease, such as at this facility at Werribee in Melbourne** *(Racing Photos)*

track cyclist. Different countries have import restrictions, so horses have to spend a couple of weeks in designated quarantine stables before leaving and after they arrive, but this is not something that the animal will notice, as it has an identical routine and is able to go outside to be exercised.

▼ **Racehorses travel first class all the way** *(Luck Greayer Bloodstock Shipping Ltd)*

Important British training centres

Newmarket

It is not just because of its tradition that Newmarket is the most important racing area in Britain. It is home to around 2,500 horses in training, the vast majority of them being Flat horses, with many more at various stages of their career.

What marks Newmarket out is its facilities. The public gallops, owned by the Jockey Club, consist of 2,500 acres of ancient heathland maintained by a large team of full-time ground staff. The gallops are predominantly in two areas – one to the west of the town where the famous racecourse is, and one to the east called Bury Side, where most of the significant stables are situated. Each has various

▼ **Newmarket Heath** (*Emma Berry*)

artificial surface training tracks designed to suit different requirements, some level and some uphill, while the different grass gallops are only open at certain times of year. The Jockey Club maintains that no area of turf is used more than once a year and much are used every two years, with new strips opened when appropriate.

Gallops are open at certain times and, with many of more than 60 trainers having their premises inside the town, there are as many horses as cars at some points in the morning. There are specific safety walkways along many roads, but it is still necessary to cross the traffic at some junctions. Most trainers have well-established routines of which gallops they will use at what time, and it all seems to work itself out, even if there can be queues for the most popular ones.

On a bright spring morning, the place to watch horses

working is overlooking the town on Warren Hill and quite a few enthusiasts will try to spot the stars of the future there, even though they are not easy to identify among groups in the same stable coats. One of the artificial Polytrack training surfaces here is passed over by around 16,000 horses every month and rises sharply uphill towards the end. Flanked by woods, it seems to capture a ritual seemingly unchanged over centuries.

With so many horses, Newmarket is also home to a huge number of stable staff and various other industries associated with the sport. The town's other claim to fame – and completely unrelated – is its sausages. The pork banger can be made by only three butchers and has been awarded Protected Geographical Indication (PGI) status, although the two main shops, Musk's and Powters, keep their recipes so secret they refuse to divulge them.

Lambourn

Although widely regarded as the main centre of jumpers, Lambourn has just as many good Flat horses trained in its environs. Part of the Berkshire downs, it is commonly known as 'the Valley of the Racehorse', home to around 1,500 of them, and more than 30 training establishments. As the village itself has a population of only 4,000, this is a pretty high ratio, and there will be talk of horses in all of its pubs.

Horses began being trained around Lambourn in the 19th century due to its well-drained and favourable grassland, and it mushroomed with the advent of the railways. A far more modern pulling point is that its proximity to the M4 motorway means that London, as well as most of the significant racecourses, can be accessed in around an hour.

There are a number of stables that have their own land for gallops, stretching outwards towards some Bronze Age burial mounds known as the Seven Barrows, but 500 acres are now managed by the Jockey Club, including 14 miles of grass and artificial gallops. It works similarly to Newmarket – trainers pay a fee to use the facilities and usually have acknowledged times in the morning at which they arrive. Most are to the north of the village in an area known as Mandown.

The gallops are also available to trainers outside the area that might only have more rudimentary facilities and want to sharpen up their horse before a race with a more serious exercise.

Among Lambourn's most celebrated residents has been Jenny Pitman, who became the first woman to train the Grand National winner when Corbiere galloped to victory in 1983. Nicky Henderson and his mentor Fred Winter both claimed multiple champion jump trainer titles from the village.

A few miles east of Lambourn, towards the Ridgeway, is another racehorse base. West Ilsley Stables used to be owned by the Queen until it was sold to Mick Channon, a former England international footballer who became a successful trainer.

▲ Lambourn, 'the Valley of the Racehorse'

▼ A frosty morning on the gallops in Lambourn

Training around the world

The training process works quite differently from country to country and from continent to continent. In most of Europe it will usually be possible for horses to be taken from their stable to the races and back either within the day, or from staying a night or two with their groom at the racecourse stables.

In more minor European racing powers, including those in Scandinavia, Spain and out towards the centre and east of the continent, horses become used to frequent and longer travel. There are not always enough suitable races for the best horses and they are required to test themselves abroad, as well as opening up the opportunity of picking up greater prize money. Just as in football, where the giants pluck star talent from the minnows, promising horses around the world are being monitored by agents and eventually end up racing on a more significant stage.

In larger countries such as Australia and America, the racing year is quite seasonal. While the low-grade horses will race at a local level and remain at home, the more important meetings will be staged in certain states at certain times of the year. It is too far to be moving back and forth for one race so a large squad will be taken across the country to a temporary base somewhere else, usually at a racecourse.

In Hong Kong and Singapore, which both have lively racing scenes but very little space, all the horses are based in dedicated training centres next to the racecourses and such is the heat that many stables are air-conditioned. In Japan there are two centres based out in the country where every horse is prepared before being transported for an hour or so to the tracks, which are nearly all based right in the city.

Training techniques vary around the world and those with aspirations of becoming a trainer usually make it part of their

education to spend at least a few months as an assistant overseas, in order to broaden their knowledge.

Visiting a stable

It is mainly only those who own a racehorse that get the chance of an individual visit to see the horses at home, but there are occasions when stables welcome in the public. The main British training centres of Newmarket, Lambourn, Epsom and the two Yorkshire hubs of Malton and Middleham all have an open day at different points during the year to raise money for charity. Most of the stables in the towns allow access for people to see and pat the horses, as well as arranging various competitions and demonstrations.

Many stables elsewhere hold their own charity open days too, while there are companies that also organise private breakfast mornings to see the horses exercise. There is always the chance on these open days that someone new might walk through the gates and decide they want to buy a horse, but the main purpose is really to give something back, engaging seasoned fans and children alike. The impression they always leave is how the horses live in luxury and how devoted the members of staff are to them.

▲ Visiting a stable always feels like a privilege – even if you are an owner

▼ Horses are given an away day at Muizenberg in Cape Town, South Africa

Famous trainers

Vincent O'Brien

No trainer has excelled in both divisions of racing at the level of this Irishman. After taking over from his late father Dan, he first specialised in the jumps and achieved astonishing success in the late '40s and early '50s, winning the Cheltenham Gold Cup three years in a row with Cottage Rake and the Grand National successively with three different horses. Later, he turned his attention to the more lucrative Flat and was just as dominant, taking all English and Irish Classics multiple times. After his retirement in 1993, the Ballydoyle, County Tipperary stable he built up almost from scratch was handed over to Aidan O'Brien (no relation), who has continued its pre-eminence.

Sir Henry Cecil

Something of a failure at school, Henry Cecil was a genius when it came to training. From the mid-'70s to the early '90s, he was virtually unbeatable and won all of Britain's major races multiple times. Although aristocratic in bearing, Cecil was popular with everyone in racing because of his honesty, friendliness and dandyish dress sense. Warren Place, his famous stable in Newmarket, was not only full of brilliant Thoroughbreds, but it was a garden full of Cecil's favourite roses and even had a pea plant germinated from some seeds taken from Tutankhamun's tomb by a relative of his stepfather. Cecil's results waned as he battled with stomach cancer but, before his death in 2013, he returned to the big time with Frankel, his unbeaten champion.

▼ Henry Cecil and jockey Steve Cauthen were an almost unbeatable combination in the 1980s

Bart Cummings

Despite being a chronic asthmatic and allergic to horses, Bart Cummings became the greatest-ever Australian trainer and a national icon. Born in Adelaide in 1927, he learned from his father, also a trainer, and was operating himself by the age of 26. He was to dominate racing across the country and particularly Australia's most famous race, the Melbourne Cup, which he won a remarkable 12 times. Not only did he carry the Olympic torch and have his face appear on a postage stamp, he was also given a state funeral when he died in 2015.

Andre Fabre

Small in stature but a giant of the Turf, Andre Fabre has monopolised French racing since the mid-1980s. A qualified lawyer and leading jump jockey in his time, he too first trained horses over fences before settling on the Flat. Fabre was something of a pioneer at running horses overseas, taking big prizes in America in the 1980s, even if he is best known for his numerous victories in the Prix de l'Arc de Triomphe. From his stables in Chantilly, he has won all of the British Classics and racegoers always pay close attention to any runners he takes across the Channel.

Martin Pipe

The son of a Somerset bookmaker who rewrote the art of jump training in Britain during the 1990s. Unconventional and with a constantly buzzing mind, Pipe was basically self-taught and embraced interval training with his horses – shorter, high-intensity exercises that got his runners far fitter than the old-fashioned style of most of his peers. He was also a pathfinder in blood testing, constantly searching for reasons why horses ran well or badly. It won him 15 champion trainer titles and the likes of the Grand National and Champion Hurdle.

▶ Martin Pipe broke new ground when it came to training jumpers

Aftercare of racehorses

Most racehorses are ready for retirement by the time they reach their teenage years; for most, simply because they have become slower, for others because it becomes hard to find suitable races for them to run in. Frequent injuries can curtail careers at a far earlier stage.

Whilst they almost all enjoy the routine of being in the stable, going out for exercise, the regular attention and a few races each year, for some horses the problem becomes psychological. They become older, wiser and occasionally trickier, deciding that going racing seems too much like hard work.

After the end of their racing career, a horse cannot switch immediately into relaxed mode and take out the golf clubs. There is a gradual transition process at the stable as it winds down from an intensive training regime, and is weaned off high-energy feed. Horses have different characters and only some will be happy spending the rest of their time out in a field with perhaps a few sheep for company. Lots like to be busy and need something different to do.

Often this is the prerogative of the trainer or owner, but charities such as Retraining of Racehorses, Moorcroft, Greatwood and HEROS work hard to find new employment for former racers, and luckily there have been many success stories. Thanks to their obedience, racehorses have been able to learn other equestrian pursuits from the speed and agility of playing polo to the discipline of dressage. There are other opportunities for them to live at riding schools, or find private owners simply looking for a nice horse to take out for a daily hack.

Thoroughbreds have even been able to make their mark in other elite-level equestrian disciplines and have been proving increasingly popular in eventing, where the price of specifically bred horses is also beyond the means of most.

Summon Up The Blood, who won three times on the Flat in Britain in 2008, took to his new sport so well that he competed at the 2016 Rio Olympics under his Brazilian rider Carlos Parro!

◥ Ex-racehorses can go on to do a number of different things. Star jumper Monet's Garden went on to win numerous showing classes

▶ Denman went into hunting and team chasing in his retirement, still retaining plenty of enthusiasm

The jockey

Preparing a horse to be in peak form for a race is the responsibility of the trainer and their staff but there is nothing more they can do once the horse has reached the start of a race. The jockey might have been issued with instructions, but it is down to them to carry out the correct tactics. Not only must the jockey have strength and polished riding technique, they need to be able to handle the pressure if their horse is expected to win. A cool head is vital, as split-second decisions often have to be made at high speed.

Becoming a jockey

It is not an obvious career path and is no different to becoming any other type of professional sportsperson, in that the cream will rise to the top and many will be left along the wayside. The way in which jockeys are recruited has changed, and gone are the Victorian days when a boy might be sent from the inner city to work for a stable simply because he was small and there were no further vacancies for chimney sweeps.

Most jockeys do tend to have been riding since childhood, either from an equestrian connection or from having a rural background and going through gymkhanas, pony clubs and maybe even some showjumping. There is then a natural progression towards working in a racing stable and riding racehorses before applying for a licence.

It is not the only way, though, and plenty of successful jockeys do not have a racing background at all. The British Racing School (BRS) in Newmarket and the Northern Racing College (NRC) in Doncaster offer a variety of courses and scholarships, some of which are for complete beginners. Both institutions are so well regarded that they are used to qualify jockeys by some overseas racing jurisdictions.

The life of a jockey is tough, rising early to partner horses in exercise before heading to the races in the afternoon and not least surviving on a strict diet. Many remain attached to one stable and ride mostly those horses, while others operate in a freelance capacity. The freelance must build up relationships with different trainers and owners, and often travel to various stables in a morning in order to show willing and secure rides.

If they remain fit and healthy, a Flat jockey could easily continue riding into his or her 50s. A jump jockey is more susceptible to falls and is not likely to last beyond 40. Some will continue as work riders, or take on training or different roles within racing, but it can be difficult to find a different career, particularly if the jockey has little formal education. Britain is fortunate enough to have the Jockeys Education & Training Scheme (JETS), a charity that has helped former riders diversify into occupations of all types.

Going to school

Unless they have outstanding talent that shines through straight away, budding jockeys first have to take steps up the ladder as members of stable staff.

A common first step in Britain is a diploma in racehorse care at the BRS or the NRC, while there are similar qualifications available from the Racing Academy and Centre of Education

▶ **Students at the British Racing School are given a thorough experience of the sport** *(Tattersalls)*

▲ British Racing School students have plenty of time to work on their riding *(BRS)*

(RACE) in Ireland. The BRS diploma is open to those between 16 and 22. This is an 18-month course that (unusually) guarantees a job in a stable to all those who complete it to the required standard. Trainers are always on the lookout for new employees, and taking them from the BRS or NRC means that they are receiving someone who already knows what the requirements will be. People can do these courses even if they have not ridden before, provided they have shown a willingness to learn in their interview.

The main schemes involve a few weeks of residential tuition at the centre. Students will be kept busy with practical work – mucking out, grooming and feeding horses – as well as receiving instruction on riding them. For some, it will be the same growing-up process as for anyone going to a college or university as they acquire life skills, live away from home and learn to manage their finances. Students will also learn about nutrition and first aid.

From there it will be on to an actual racing yard, in an agreed location somewhere around the country, where the real work begins, and future jockeys will be given horses to look after and an opportunity to finesse their riding in morning exercise. They will either sink or swim from this stage. The part of the course that involves staying at the centre costs around £500, including accommodation and food, although some concessions can be made. There are various levels of courses, depending upon age and experience, which can easily be discussed with them.

Pony racing

Irish jockeys are world-renowned because many have been riding in intense competition since they were children. Pony racing is the proving ground, where nearly every top Irish rider has cut their teeth. Some meetings, such as the Dingle Derby in picturesque County Kerry, attract huge crowds as well as frenzied betting. Latterly, there has been a formal attempt to replicate the system in Britain in order to identify and nurture more of the jockeys of the future.

Pony races have been held informally, often as part of the attractions at British point-to-point races, for many years. They are open to riders aged between 9 and 16, provided they have been to a training day, attended Pony Club rallies or hunted with a recognised pack of hounds.

The races are usually between six furlongs and a mile and are categorised by the size of the horse, with races for those of a maximum size of 138cm and 148cm tall. Ages of jockeys are fairly mixed, but ideally the older the rider, the bigger the pony. This should give youngsters the full experience, not only from

◄ Jockeys of the future gain experience in the pony-racing scene going out and performing in front of a crowd, but also for holding their own, making decisions during a race and riding a finish.

When talking ponies, these are not the tiny little Shetland variety. They are far more like mini racehorses; trained up, extremely fast and often quite expensive. Many of the riders are children of those involved in the industry, so there are usually some familiar surnames.

Since 2004, the Pony Racing Authority (PRA) has been staging a series on British racecourses for riders aged between 11 and 16. Often these are before the Thoroughbred races start, or occasionally they are meetings in their own right. It is already paying off, with a few pony-racing champions making the grade as fully fledged jockeys.

For parents, pony racing is clearly going to be another expensive pursuit, but the PRA has been attempting to make it more accessible to all, with taster sessions organised around the country as well as a youth training scheme.

Becoming an apprentice or conditional jockey

It is up to the trainer to decide whether they think someone they employ is ready or good enough to ride in races. If they are, then they must apply to be an apprentice (for Flat racing) or a conditional (for jump racing). These are essentially the same thing, apart from some differences in the percentage of their prize money and riding fees they get to keep before they become fully fledged jockeys.

An apprentice or conditional licence is open to riders aged between 16 and 26 years old, who are in full-time paid employment with a trainer. The candidate must apply to the BHA and then attend another five-day course at one of the racing schools, as well as undergoing a medical examination and meeting fitness standards.

The rider has to prove that they are capable of riding a racehorse at speed, and are assessed on a simulator. Flat jockeys will have to demonstrate that they are familiar with using the starting stalls, while jump jockeys will have to negotiate practice hurdles and fences. They are given further lessons on nutrition, sports science and the rules of racing.

A conditional or apprentice jockey must be employed by a licensed trainer, but is allowed to take rides for other trainers. As they are learning their trade, they are entitled to take some extra weight off their horse to compensate for their inexperience in most types of races, known as a claim.

It is a dilemma for both trainers and punters when considering a horse that is to be ridden by an apprentice or conditional. The weight allowance is supposed to even up the scales between beginners and hardened riders. Word spreads very quickly when a talented new apprentice hits the scene, as that claim suddenly becomes sought after. If a trainer has a

▲ Riders must gain experience on the gallops before they can think about riding in a race

▲ Qualifying to become a jockey is not only about riding *(Northern Racing College)*

▲ Apprentice jockeys will not receive their licence until they have reached the right standard *(Northern Racing College)*

horse that they think might win an important handicap but is still carrying a lot of weight, they might choose a claiming jockey to give it a better chance.

However, it must be remembered that some of these jockeys are still very young and are either physically weaker or less accustomed to the track craft and tactics that are required. As much as they might have been riding horses in exercise for years, nearly all jockeys remember their first rides in public being over in a flash before they realised how far they had travelled or what they were supposed to be doing.

Once they reach the 75 or 95 winner mark, these jockeys lose their claim and are on a level playing field with the big guns. This, as happens in many sports when junior stars have to graduate

to all-aged competition, is when some will fall by the wayside, and some jockeys become less attractive propositions. It is up to the trainer that employs the apprentice to guide their career and ensure their wards take it step by step and do not rush through their claim just because other trainers start offering them rides.

Amateur jockeys

Not all jockeys want to turn professional, at least immediately. Amateur riders are not paid for their rides and do not have to be employed by a stable but are still required to attend a short course and prove capability and fitness in the saddle before receiving a permit. They must also become a member of the Amateur Jockeys Association. Many youngsters will opt for this route first, as they can start off in races confined to other amateurs, either on the Flat or over jumps, and might opt to become a conditional or apprentice after they have got themselves going.

Others choose to remain amateur because race riding is a hobby away from another job, such as Sam Waley-Cohen, who won the 2011 Cheltenham Gold Cup but also established a chain of dental practices. Amateurs also receive an allowance until they have ridden a certain amount of winners. Very few ride regularly against the professionals and will have a Mr, Miss or Mrs against their name in the racecard to denote this criterion.

Being an amateur also allows a rider to continue in point-to-point races as well as riding in normal 'Rules' races. There is an amateurs' Derby at Epsom, as well as several sought-after events at the Cheltenham Festival, which are exclusive to amateurs and where the best of them are in high demand. In

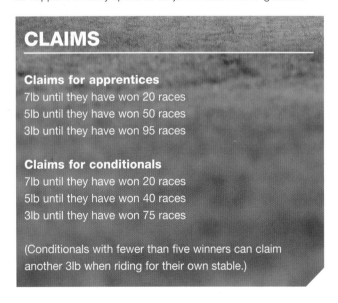

CLAIMS

Claims for apprentices
7lb until they have won 20 races
5lb until they have won 50 races
3lb until they have won 95 races

Claims for conditionals
7lb until they have won 20 races
5lb until they have won 40 races
3lb until they have won 75 races

(Conditionals with fewer than five winners can claim another 3lb when riding for their own stable.)

▶ Sam Waley-Cohen became the first amateur rider to win the Cheltenham Gold Cup for 30 years when Long Run prevailed in 2011

Ireland, where point-to-pointing is a big shop window for selling horses to proper jump racing, the top amateurs are said to be paid informally to ride and some make as good a living out of the game as the pros.

Female jockeys

At some stage in the future, female jockeys will be so accepted and successful that there will not be separate sections in books like this. Nonetheless, it is still important to point out that racing, along with other equestrian events, is one of the few sports in which both sexes compete against each other on a level playing field.

This was certainly not always the case in racing. It was not until 1969 that Diane Crump had to be given a police escort and steered through a jeering crowd to become the first woman to ride in a professional race in America, and not until 1972 that Meriel Tufnell was the first to win a race in Britain under the rules of racing.

The milestones have gradually been ticked off. Geraldine Rees rode in the Grand National in 1977 and Julie Krone made history in 1993 by winning the Belmont Stakes, one of the three stages of America's famous Triple Crown. The percentage of female professional jockeys is not in line with the large amount of women that work as stable staff but increased to around a seventh through the 2010s in Britain. In Australia, where it is up to a quarter, women have already won national titles and Michelle Payne has claimed the country's most important race, the Melbourne Cup. Growth has been more noticeable in Flat racing than over jumps, but the Irish women Katie Walsh and Nina Carberry have claimed races at the Cheltenham Festival and become authentic crowd favourites.

Prejudices do exist among the more old-fashioned brigade of racehorse trainers about using female jockeys, but these are thankfully eroding fast. Many female apprentices have also been able to get opportunities because they can do lighter weights than heavier male colleagues.

Although argued to be at a disadvantage in terms of strength, female jockeys have succeeded due to having the variety of attributes required to make a career in the saddle. There were similar barriers to women becoming trainers until a few decades ago but the likes of Jenny Pitman, who saddled the winner of the Grand National in 1983, and Gai Waterhouse, often referred to as 'the first lady of Australian racing', have ensured that discussion of their gender has long been immaterial.

◀ **Irishwoman Nina Carberry has raised the bar in recent years with her jump racing successes** (Patrick McCann)

Riding in a race

Knowing the horse

It is considered helpful to a jockey if they have ridden a horse before, either in exercise or in a previous race, as they will know if it has a quirk – perhaps being particularly enthusiastic, a careless jumper, or only likely to win if delivered to the front very late. A jockey that has a formal arrangement with a trainer, rather than one who is freelance, will try to get to know each horse at least briefly in the stable.

The jockey's information is helpful to a trainer, and vice versa, and the individual feedback from each rider helps to build up a picture of what type of horse it is. A good jockey ought to have a fair idea of what kind of distance, ground and track the horse will be best suited to, by judging the way it moves and responds. This helps build up a rapport between jockey, trainer and owner.

It does not pay to be solely reliant on an experience from the gallops, which are pieces of controlled exercise designed to help the horse's progression. With ten other jockeys out there in opposition, a race makes the experience very different, and a jockey must not go out on the racecourse with a blinkered view on the way the race must be run in order for them to win. Many top riders have also won big races without even seeing the horse before they have jumped on its back in the paddock.

Horses can be very different beasts when in competition mode compared with how they behave at home. They can look like Pegasus on the gallops and a sloth on the track, leaving trainer and jockey scratching their heads as to what has gone wrong. Alternatively, they can be sluggish and uninterested in their morning work, but come alive once racing.

In maiden races for horses that have run very few or no times before, the rumours and information from the stable seep into the betting market. News of a horse that has been burning up the gallops travels fast and bookmakers will not take chances of offering long odds on an unknown quantity that customers are queuing up to have a bet on.

Deciding the tactics

Jockeys will spend time before each race analysing the previous performances and running styles of their rivals, and sometimes watching replays. Their first focus is working out whether there are many others in the race that are likely to lead or at least head towards the front. This will give them a fair idea how everything is going to pan out, and where they should be

▲ Feedback between trainer and rider is very important when assessing a horse

▼ Tactics are decided between the trainer and jockey

placing themselves in the pack in order to give their horse the best possible chance of winning.

In a short-distance Flat race, jockeys will look at the starting stall numbers their rivals have been assigned. If there are a number of fast horses clustered on a particular side of the track, they might need to move their horse across the track to join them as soon as the race is started.

Some horses have an instinct to lead and run best out on their own, whilst others are more suited to following in behind and using their finishing kick. This is often a trial-and-error process. In a race in which none have shown an inclination to set the pace, there is an opportunity for someone to make a brisk start and steal a valuable advantage. Jockeys are employed to keep cool under pressure and be able to make quick and sensible decisions during the race.

Once they have 'weighed out' and gone to join the trainer and owner in the paddock, last-minute tactics will be decided. Some trainers and owners will be very particular as to how they want their horse to be ridden. If the horse gets beaten, it at least makes the jockey's life easier when they come back from the track if they can say they were only following the instructions they were given. Most trainers are more relaxed and might just relay any last-minute important information. They trust the jockey to know what they are doing and leave the tactics to them.

The race itself

Once the jockey has been given the 'leg-up' by the trainer, jumped into the saddle and let loose to head to the start, they are all on their own. Races do not always develop like a computer simulation and tactics quickly go out of the window.

Jason Weaver, now a television broadcaster, rode more than 1000 Flat winners in Britain, including the Gold Cup at Royal Ascot and the 2000 Guineas at Newmarket, and would have a better idea than most:

"From a jockey's perspective, a massive percentage is instinct from the minute you break out of the gate to the initial tempo of the race and the conditions of the day.

We always talk about the finish, but the start is so important – there are so many races that are lost in the early part. It is about finding a rhythm, and the way you hold the reins gives them confidence. If I sat on your back and started pulling you around and messing about, you are not going to go very quickly. The less of a hindrance you are, the better.

If you attached an 8st weight onto a horse's back and had it perfectly still and balanced, the horse could reach its optimum speed over two furlongs at its absolute fastest. If the weight was loosely shackled, bouncing around and manoeuvring all over the place, its speed could be significantly slower as it would be fighting against all that weight.'

When a horse is running along energetically and smoothly, with the jockey having their hands low making a good contact with the animal via the bit and the reins, it will often be described as being 'on the bridle'. When the horse begins to tire and go 'off the bridle' it backs off a little and the jockey has to crouch a little lower, adjust the reins and start to drive the horse forward towards the finish. Riders only really resort to the whip in the concluding stages of a race as the final form of encouragement, so if they start using it earlier, it is not a promising sign as to their prospects."

The sign of a good horse

Some horses are, by nature, lazy and will need more encouragement and attention during the race. If they were let loose, though, they would continue to gallop along with the herd, as no one wants to get left behind. Jason Weaver says the feeling of being on a top-quality horse is very different to riding an average one:

"If you are lucky enough to sit on a really good one, where everything is mechanically in the right place, it will glide over the ground no matter what sort of conditions you are on.

It's like driving in a top-of-the-range car that doesn't feel a bump in the road. Everything is easy and they've got plenty left when you want it. The best ones are usually very intelligent; they relax and they listen to you.

A lot of the time you will know very soon after you get on

◀ **Down at the start, the jockey is left to formulate a plan, but much of it is down to instinct** *a good horse. They are just good athletes. It's just the way they look and the way they move, there's a different feel. It can sometimes be difficult to get the most suitable racing distance right, because they have got so much natural speed and still some kick at the end when they finish. Some of the best I rode would be quick enough to win a sprint but also over a much longer trip."*

After the race

Once the jockey dismounts, they have to take the saddle off and return to the weighing room with it. First, though, there is a debrief with the owner and trainer. It is up to the jockey to talk them through how the race went and what went right or wrong. Usually there is valuable information to be learned about how the horse handled the ground and the distance. Sometimes this requires an element of diplomacy to a disappointed owner who has paid a king's ransom for an unproven horse and is coming to terms with the fact that it might not actually be a superstar. The onus is on the jockey to be helpful and encouraging but honest with their feedback. Talking to owners and explaining the performance articulately is part of the advice young jockeys receive in their racing education.

What can a jockey earn?

For the elite few, in Flat and jump racing, there are handsome earnings to be made as a jockey. There could be six-figure 'retainers' from owners or trainers to ride their horses, contracts to ride overseas during the winter and plenty of prizes to be earned. Top jockeys such as the American John Velazquez and the Japanese Yutaka Take, hugely successful from their early twenties through to their late forties, have had their cut of hundreds of millions in race prizes.

A British Flat jockey earns a set fee per ride of £120, paid by the horse's owner via Weatherbys. As a jump jockey, who is arguably putting themselves at greater risk due to the threat of falls, the fee is around £165. Popular riders in Britain might get a ride in every race at the meeting, or even head on to an evening meeting from an afternoon one, perhaps riding in ten races on a good day, so it clearly adds up.

From prize money, depending on the race, a jump jockey will earn 8.5–9% of the winning purse, while it is set at 6.9% on the Flat. In both codes, the jockey will get 3.5% of any prize money if they finish in the other places. There are earnings to be made from riding horses in exercise and many will have sponsors for the likes of their car and their breeches, or have some media work.

However, there are percentages to be given to their agent and valet, and there are further deductions to the Professional Jockeys' Association, for insurance, for physiotherapists and for

▲ A top-class racehorse will do everything easily

administrative fees. An investigation by the *Racing Post* in 2017 estimated that an average Flat and jumps jockey in Britain riding between 200 and 300 races would earn around £27,000 from the sport, so clearly many are not even pulling that in.

Britain is unique in the number of meetings spread around the country, which almost all jockeys are likely to visit. This means huge amounts of time in the car (only a select few have access to a helicopter or private plane). Most jockeys will cover 50,000 miles in a year, but at least the fuel and vehicle upkeep is tax deductible for the self-employed businessperson.

▼ The life of a jockey is a very busy one
(www.focusonracing.com)

Clerk of the Scales

The agent

The life of a jockey is hectic enough to need a bit of help. Chief among those is their agent, who is responsible for booking their rides. An agent's life is spent on the telephone, either fielding calls from those looking to use their jockeys' services, or hunting around for other rides.

The agent's aim is to get the jockey as many rides and winners as possible, as usually they work to a 10% commission on whatever they earn from the job. It is a pretty complicated business, involving advanced planning through the week, studying the advanced entries and seeing where the best chances will be.

Firstly the agent factors into account any ties their jockey has with owners and trainers, as riding their horses takes priority. After that, they can start looking at the other races at that meeting, finding trainers with whom the jockey has some sort of allegiance or connection, and ringing them to see if they are interested in using them.

Jockeys put their trust in their agent to make the right decisions for them, and strong relationships develop; legendary jump jockey Tony McCoy, for example, was allied with Dave Roberts throughout his career.

The job requires an intimate knowledge of racing form, considering the weather through the week and the likelihood of certain horses running in races, as well as the sort of weights they will carry – not to mention the time it takes to travel between racecourses if their rider is attempting to get from an afternoon meeting to an evening meeting. 'A lot of it is luck,' admitted one leading agent. 'Also, you're just trying to upset as few people as possible.'

Positions will constantly change through the week and even in the minutes leading up to the declaration time of a race, with owners changing their mind on which jockey they want, or trainers deciding they will run a horse at a different destination. Some of the top agents can have a stable of more than a dozen jockeys, with numerous phones on their desk ringing non-stop, along with antisocial and very long hours. When one of their riders wins the Derby or the Grand National, though, there is a good payoff.

Valets

One of the principal figures in a jockey's working life is their valet, who organises all of their equipment in the weighing room on raceday. A few master valets and their teams of helpers look after the entire riding community, travelling around with them from track to track, and they usually ferry around the jockey's kit, apart from the changeable racing colours and cap and perhaps their whip.

Arriving a few hours in advance, they will lay out sets of clean breeches, underwear, socks and towels, polish up their boots and check that the helmets, saddles and goggles are safe and usable.

Once racing begins, it gets even busier, as they start liaising with the trainers and their representatives, receiving their sets of silk colours and helping to prepare saddles according to the weights the horses are set to carry. With only a few minutes between races, the most in-demand jockeys need to have the right coloured outfits hanging up on their pegs ready to be changed into for the next event. Positions in the weighing room are decided by seniority, and years spent with their charges means that the valet has a fairly intimate knowledge of the jockey's requirements.

A valet will often have to come up with practical solutions to problems during the meeting and then scoop everything up and into the van, washing and cleaning overnight to ensure everything is sparkling again by the time of the next day's meeting.

There is a general agreement that a British valet gets 10% of a jockey's first riding fee per day, 7.5% for the second and 5% from the third – it works out at around £15 a race. The valet is relieving them of a fair chunk of wages but is someone that they would struggle to survive without. Some are ex-jockeys themselves. The late John Buckingham, who became world-famous when steering Foinavon past a pile-up of every other runner in the 1967 Grand National and went on to win at 100–1, was the master valet in British weighing rooms for 30 years after he retired.

▶ A valet looks after and sets out all the racing kit a jockey needs during the day

Kit

Helmet

Only certain helmets or 'skull caps' comply with tight safety regulations and are much the same as those used by many hobby riders. They must have a chinstrap under the jaw that undoes with a buckle. The silk cap worn on top of it during a race can easily be changed, but it does sometimes come off during a race.

▶ **LAS JC Star Jockey helmet** *(Gibson Saddlers)*

Body protector

All jockeys wear a body protector, which must also meet official safety standards. Racing's versions are incredibly lightweight and ultra-modern, consisting of sections of protective foam panels for shock absorption. They are also adjustable and well ventilated, given they would be rather sweaty on a hot day, and jockeys usually go for a lightweight lycra top underneath.

▶ **ProRace body protector** *(Gibson Saddlers)*

Breeches

Made of polyester and incredibly light – the main product weights 170g and there is an even more updated version weighing just 80g. A jockey will have a few pairs, including a more waterproof set if the weather is awful. Most equipment

▶ **Ornella Prosperi race breeches** *(Gibson Saddlers)*

comes from Italian company Ornella or Hyland from Australia. Top riders have sponsorship deals and, as well as their names, their breeches carry branding along the legs.

Whip

The old stiff leather whips were long outlawed in organised racing nations on grounds of horse welfare. Instead, they have a long shaft of cushioned, shock-absorbing padding on the end that is used on the horse. It does not cause any pain – find one and smack it on a human hand and it does not even sting – and instead makes a popping sound that will urge a horse on for greater effort.

New whips are the result of extensive scientific testing and are strictly regulated – they must be a maximum of 68cm for jump jockeys and 70cm for Flat jockeys, to provide slightly more flexibility, and weigh no more than 160g.

▶ **Flat racing whip** *(Gibson Saddlers)*

Goggles

A jockey will have a few sets of goggles, which are inexpensive and elasticated so that they fit over the helmet. They do not only protect the eyes from flying mud in poor conditions, but come in a variety of shades so that glare is never an issue. On a very bad day a jockey may wear several pairs at once, peeling

▲ Several pairs of goggles are needed in the mud

them off during the race as they get covered with mud and harder to see through.

▶ Gibson racewear goggles
(Gibson Saddlers)

Boots

Normal riding boots might be made from leather but racing boots are made from patent synthetic materials. A jockey will have three or four pairs, including an almost paper-thin set for light weights.

▶ A jockey will have a few sets of boots at the races, depending on the weight they need to make

▼ Ornella Prosperi jockey boot
(Gibson Saddlers)

Saddle

A jockey will have at least four different saddles in their kit bag. An in-demand jockey will have lots of rides and there is plenty of swapping around of the saddle, weighing, and getting their saddle put onto their horse for the next race. They usually have

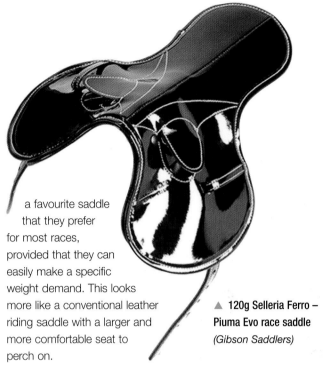

a favourite saddle that they prefer for most races, provided that they can easily make a specific weight demand. This looks more like a conventional leather riding saddle with a larger and more comfortable seat to perch on.

▲ 120g Selleria Ferro – Piuma Evo race saddle
(Gibson Saddlers)

For those struggling to make a weight, there are now saddles weighing just 120g, made of carbon fibre and other modern materials. The actual seat might only be 28cm and looks like something a tiny child might use. These are more suitable for Flat jockeys, who are perched precariously and high up in the saddle, whereas a jump jockey needs to use their legs more and needs more substantial equipment. Stirrups, which are usually associated with being made of steel or aluminium, can even be made of a durable plastic if a jockey is desperate to save a few more grams.

▼ Top jockeys will have their names stitched onto custom-made saddles

Injuries

Accidents happen all the time with horses, whether exercising them at home or if they get upset in the paddock. For the most part, though, injuries are picked up by jockeys in races. Over jumps, the rule of thumb has been that you will hit the deck one in every 13 times, through the horse falling itself, by being unseated from the saddle or by being brought down by another. It is for this reason that horse racing is the only sport where the competitors are directly followed by an ambulance.

A jump jockey is at least semi-prepared for a fall at each obstacle, as they straighten their legs and lean back in the saddle, but actually landing rolled up into a ball must be instinctive as everything happens so quickly. Although horses coming from behind will actually do their best to avoid those on the floor, there is still a chance of getting kicked.

◀▼ **Jump jockeys could take a fall around once in every 13 rides, so must always be prepared**

Falls on the Flat are rarer, but are potentially more serious. They usually happen when a horse gets injured or receives interference from others, either from clipping heels with those in front and tripping over or getting squeezed. These are happening at a faster speed, the jockeys are not expecting it, and the other runners are usually more closely packed together.

While they wear some protective equipment, injuries are frequent and vary from bumps, bruises and fractured collarbones, which should not take too long to heal, to serious breaks of legs, arms, backs and necks.

Jockeys are notoriously tough and do not want someone else riding their best horses, so will endeavour to be back as quickly as possible. However, they are supposed to inform a medical officer of any problems immediately. After more serious illnesses or injuries, they will not only have to be cleared by a specialist but then see the racing medical department to be passed fit to ride.

As in other sports, concussion is an issue that is being treated with more importance. Jockeys that have suffered this will undergo a stand-down period and have to take several neuro-psychological tests before they are declared ready to return to action.

Ruby Walsh

Irishman Ruby Walsh is one of the most successful jump jockeys of all time, winning all of Cheltenham's great prizes and the Grand National, as well as valuable prizes in America, Japan, France and at home. The nature of his job, though, means he has suffered some horrendous injuries through his career.

▲ Ruby Walsh (left) is congratulated after another big-race win

Ruby Walsh's injuries

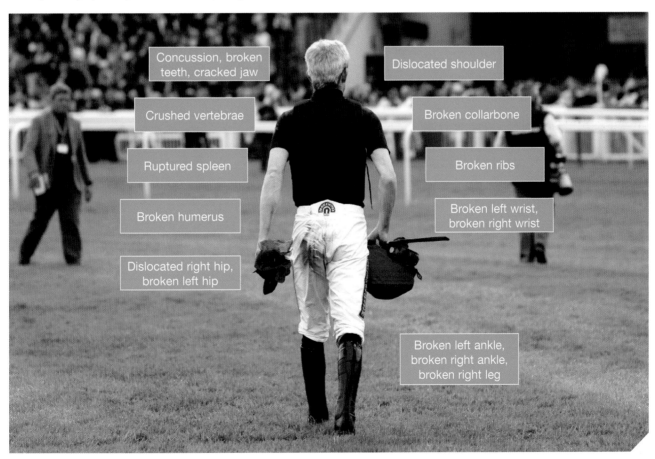

Concussion, broken teeth, cracked jaw

Dislocated shoulder

Crushed vertebrae

Broken collarbone

Ruptured spleen

Broken ribs

Broken humerus

Broken left wrist, broken right wrist

Dislocated right hip, broken left hip

Broken left ankle, broken right ankle, broken right leg

Jockey care

The available help for British-based riders when they have been injured has increased dramatically in recent years and this is almost entirely due to the Injured Jockeys' Fund (IJF), which was established as a charity in 1964. It has raised millions, not only to help the rehabilitation of those working their way back towards a return to the saddle, but in supporting those whose careers have been ended. There are now specialist centres in the three major racing hubs of Newmarket, Lambourn and Malton, which have teams of specialists in sports science and therapists, as well as high-class gym facilities to bring the jockeys back to fitness. The IJF also has almoners to offer support to those around the country and can offer residential care to the seriously injured. It works closely with Racing

Welfare, another charity that was created to offer professional guidance and help to all those who work around stables and studs. More recently, a similar charity was founded in Ireland, and there are some trusts in place in other countries.

Jockeys in Britain also pay 3% of their fees to the Professional Jockeys' Association (PJA), their union, which provides a number of valuable services. For most practical help, it works with a team of physiotherapists that travel around the racecourses offering short- and long-term solutions to aches and pains. There is also a team of nutritionists and for those affected by mental health issues, the PJA works with a counselling service to provide a confidential hotline.

One of the most serious occasions when a jockey will need to call upon the union is when they have fallen foul of the authorities, perhaps when they have been handed a suspension they disagree with. If appropriate, the PJA representative will lodge an appeal at the British Horseracing Authority for them and can provide legal

▼ The Oaksey House jockey rehabilitation centre in Lambourn, named after the late Lord Oaksey (third right), was opened by IJF patron, HRH The Princess Royal, in 2009 *(IJF)*

representation or advice via its expenses scheme. The PJA is also the guardian of jockeys' commercial rights and helps them with dealing with insurance, pension plans and visas.

Diet

The requirements of a jockey are to be operating at peak level, yet under what would most likely be their natural body weight. Operating at an average weight of between eight-and-a-half and nine stone on the Flat, or between ten and eleven stone over jumps might be easy if you are only five feet tall and have a swift metabolism. Some are lucky and can eat what they like, but there have been some high-profile riders reaching nearly six feet, for whom making these weights must have been challenging.

For many years the diet of jockeys was ignored, with apocryphal stories of those surviving on only black tea and cigarettes perhaps not wholly far from the truth. Certainly, jockeys would do without breakfast or lunch and just about manage a small meal in the evening.

The use of weight-loss pills and even worse, 'flipping' or self-induced vomiting was thought to be widespread. Without names being named, it is acknowledged that the latter is still known to go on, despite the risk of dehydration, high blood pressure, dizziness and poor bone health. This is something that officials have attempted to eradicate by providing jockeys with greater access to knowledge about eating properly.

In Britain, the PJA and BHA work closely with institutions including Liverpool John Moores University and members of a full-time nutrition team tour the racecourses. Jockeys are slowly learning that they need to provide their bodies with fuel in order to control and even lose weight, and that eating small portions regularly is far more effective than once or hardly at all. They are advised to look at foods that are lower in calories and saturated fats and higher in protein and fibre.

While most are widely thought to be surviving on 1,000 calories per day – less than half the recommended allowance – they are provided with lists of recommended foods and even recipes. Most of them involve common sense, and the consumption of plenty of fruit and vegetables, green tea, chicken and fish.

Short, sharp exercises to stimulate the metabolism have also started to replace the mantra of not eating and spending hours in a hot bath or sauna, but it will take time before everyone has adopted the modern methods.

Fitness

While they might not look the most impressive of physical specimens, jockeys have come out favourably in terms of fitness when tested with other elite sportspeople. It is not only the toughness to withstand falling off, it is strength in the arms and legs to hold a horse and push it along for races that can

▲ Despite being 6ft tall, George Baker maintained his weight to be a Flat jockey with a combination of good diet and exercise *(IJF)*

last anything between one minute (a five-furlong sprint) and nine minutes (the Grand National). They also require a strong core and plenty of endurance, so most jockeys have regular exercise regimes involving circuit or weight training, running, swimming or cycling, as well as the time in the saddle.

▼ Making it as a professional jockey requires a combination of strength and fitness *(IJF)*

All British jockeys have to undertake a British Racing School standard test from a series of fundamental exercises in order to be considered for a licence. For a professional, the pass mark is 70% and for an amateur it is 65%. This involves the following:

Exercise ball leg repetitions and holds

Holding a 5kg weight and facing away from the wall with a gym ball behind the small of the back, participants will do 20 squats rolling the ball up and down the wall and then hold in the squat position with the knees bent for as long as possible.

Holding for one minute scores 50%, with 100% attained by holding for two minutes.

Wobble cushion squats

Standing with a wobble cushion under each foot, participants must bend their knees with thighs horizontal and remain in the pushing position that they would adopt on a horse.

Maintaining this pose for two minutes scores 50%, with 100% for the maximum of four minutes.

Press-up position

Adopting a press-up position on the ground, with elbows bent at 90 degrees and close to the sides, participants must hold this stance for as long as possible.

Holding for 45 seconds scores 50%, with 100% attained by holding for a minute and a half.

▼ A good sense of balance is key to becoming a top jockey *(IJF)*

Elastic band push to metronome

Sitting upright on a bench, with their knees bent at a right angle, participants must push out a heavy duty elastic band in the style they might push out a horse, keeping in time with a metronome set at 50 beats per minute.

Maintaining this exercise for one minute scores 50%, reaching two minutes scores 100%.

Leg raises to metronome

Lying on their back with arms over the shoulders holding onto something solid, participants must raise their feet to point upwards, keeping their ankles together and their legs straight, moving up and then down along to a metronome set again at 50 beats per minute.

Continuing for two minutes scores 50%, reaching four minutes scores 100%.

The plank

Locking their hands together and balancing on their elbows, participants must raise their body and straighten their legs so that they are supported by the balls of their feet and their feet are hip-distance apart. Without arching their back or sticking their bottom upwards, this position must be maintained.

Holding for two minutes scores 50%, reaching four minutes scores 100%.

Bleep test

Familiar to many from physical education lessons at school, participants must run between markers 20 metres apart up to the maximum level of 13.

The maximum level (13) scores 100%, each level below scores 10% less.

Simulator

Some jockeys will have their own mechanical horse or 'equicizer' at home to practise on, or have regular access to them. Although still relatively new technology, these have now become motorised and can have their speed adjusted from cantering up to a full-scale gallop.

The fitness test requires the jockey to push the simulator along as if they were going flat-out in a finish and follow any instructions given.

Continuing to ride satisfactorily to the assessor for two minutes scores 50%, continuing up to four minutes scores 100%.

▲ A young rider is put through her paces on the equicizer by an accredited jockey coach, Cathy Gannon *(IJF)*

Testing

Jockeys are subject to fairly rigorous scrutiny when it comes to drink and drugs use. In Britain, the sampling officers will select a meeting and every jockey will have to take and pass an alcohol breathalyser test. The threshold is 17 micrograms per 100 millimetres in breath, which is around half of the drink-driving limit. The result of even a low-key evening out the night before the race for someone who is very light in weight could result in the jockey being stood down for the day. More serious transgressions result in suspensions. The hard-drinking lifestyle of jockeys is very much of a bygone age and it is no surprise that many are now teetotal.

Next a randomly selected group of at least ten must go off and submit a urine sample, which is sent off for laboratory testing. This can, on occasion, produce a positive result. Those testing above the threshold for various stimulants and the likes of cannabis, cocaine and its various metabolites can come in for very serious punishments indeed. Some jockeys have fallen foul of the authorities in overseas jurisdictions and been handed long reciprocal bans.

Greatest ever jockeys

Fred Archer

An icon of the Victorian era, Fred Archer was British champion Flat jockey on 13 consecutive occasions between 1874 and his death in 1886, aged just 29. Archer won 21 Classics and set records that lasted for decades, despite having to travel to meetings around the country by train.

Born in Cheltenham, he was sent to become an apprentice in Newmarket aged just 11. He grew to 5ft 10in and was depicted as painfully thin, and said to be of a miserly disposition. Depressed after the loss of his wife and thought to have become delirious, he shot himself.

Remembered as an almost mystical figure of the Turf, he was loved by punters and the phrase 'Archer's up' (or Archer is aboard), meaning all is well, lasted for many years more. His ghost is thought to haunt Newmarket Heath on his grey mare, Scotch Pearl.

Lester Piggott

Still a household name in Britain and Ireland, Lester Piggott is to many the greatest jockey that ever lived. The son of a trainer, he became a teenage sensation, winning the first of nine Derbies aboard Never Say Die in 1954. He was 11-times champion and won virtually every race of consequence, often displaying a ruthless streak in deposing other jockeys to get aboard the horse he fancied in major events. His split with trainer Sir Noel Murless to team up with Vincent O'Brien not only established 'jockey power' but he was also in tune with the times, establishing Piggott as a slightly rebellious figure and breaking the traditional master-servant mould of jockey and trainer. This notoriety, together with his reputation as the 'housewives' choice' for the big races, considerably raised racing's profile at the time and went some way to changing its rather class-bound image.

After he retired and started training, Piggott was jailed for a year for tax evasion, but then made a stunning return to the saddle in 1990, winning the then massively important Breeders' Cup Mile international race in the United States within ten days of his comeback. Piggott, who was partially deaf and also lost a significant portion of an ear in a stalls accident, finally retired in 1995.

Frankie Dettori

One of the most decorated of Flat jockeys, Dettori has transcended the barriers of racing to become well known and popular in the wider world, as a television panel show regular and a restaurant owner.

The Italian arrived in Britain as a teenager and has never left, particularly breaking through in the national consciousness by winning all seven races at a showpiece meeting at Ascot in 1996, which put some bookmakers out of business. He had a long arrangement as jockey for Sheikh Mohammed, the ruler of Dubai, who has a large number of horses in Britain.

Briefly banned at the end of 2012 for taking a prohibited substance, he was to undergo a renaissance for his former mentor and the champion trainer, John Gosden, regaining his earlier confidence as well as his flamboyant style.

◀ **Lester Piggott will forever be remembered for his genius in the saddle**

▲ Italian Frankie Dettori has perhaps been British racing's greatest asset

▲ Tony 'A.P.' McCoy became the ultimate jump jockey in breaking all records

Dettori has been champion British jockey and captured races around the world, usually jumping from the saddle in the winners' enclosure, known as his flying dismount. He has probably single-handedly done more to help popularise racing in the UK than anyone since Lester Piggott.

John Francome

The most stylish and charismatic of all jockeys, Francome became champion jockey on seven occasions. Most memorable was his fourth, in 1982, when he stopped when he equalled the total of his rival Peter Scudamore, who had been sidelined through injury. Francome thought it more sporting to share the jockeys' title than win it in those circumstances.

Born in Swindon, and a successful showjumper in his youth, he learned the ropes at the nearby stable of Fred Winter, for whom he rode his only Cheltenham Gold Cup winner on Midnight Court in 1978. His other major winner came on Sea Pigeon in the 1981 Champion Hurdle.

It was Francome's horsemanship that appealed, as well as his quick wit, which he transferred into becoming perhaps the most popular television racing pundit. He invested first in fish and chip shops in Swindon and then in property and writing

racing novels, which earned him far more than he ever accrued from the saddle.

A.P. McCoy

Sir Anthony Peter McCoy is rather better known as Tony or just 'A.P.', the setter of jumps records that might never be beaten. Born in Northern Ireland, McCoy moved to England in 1994 and was champion conditional jockey that season. He was fully fledged champion the following year and retained the title 20 consecutive times, right the way up to his retirement. Relentlessly driven, he established astonishing new marks including collecting 289 winners in a season, thereby beating Sir Gordon Richards' Flat racing total, which had lasted for more than 50 years.

McCoy first formed an unbeatable combination with Martin Pipe and later teamed up with Irish owner JP McManus, who finally provided him with an elusive Grand National in 2010. The victory led to him receiving the BBC Sports Personality of the Year award. What characterised McCoy is that he was seemingly impervious to pain and damage, returning within weeks from injuries that might have kept others out for months.

The owner

There is much to dream about in having a horse running in your own racing colours, or enjoying the experience with friends, family or simply other like-minded people. There are around 8,000 registered owners in Britain, with the Racehorse Owners Association estimating that when taking syndicates and clubs into account, around 35,000 people have an involvement.

As a sole owner, you can give the horse a name and watch it progress on the gallops before it finally runs. Then your name will be in the racecard and newspapers and you might even be interviewed on racing television. You will meet a jockey and listen to the race tactics being discussed by the trainer. There are trophies to be collected, pictures to be taken and celebratory drinks to be had in the winning connections' room.

For some, there might be thousands of pounds' worth of prizes, trips around the world or even millions to be negotiated for the horse's breeding rights in the future. But hold on. It's a very expensive business to even own one horse and the law of averages dictates that it probably won't even be any good. Nonetheless, it is the thought of fun times or potential riches that encourages so many to continue buying them.

Becoming an individual owner

According to a survey by the Racehorse Owners Association in 2017 it costs, on average, around £20,000 to have a horse in training for a year, in Britain. With a Flat horse running on average seven times per year and a jumps horse five, it is well beyond the means of most people. Naturally enough, the cost will be higher to have the horse trained by a famous name in Newmarket or Lambourn, and less by a smaller practitioner.

Prize money

Owners do at least get the lion's share of the prize money, although it might not necessarily be very much unless you win the Derby. In Britain, the winning owner gets around 50% of the value of the races themselves, the second owner 20% and the third owner 10%.

Total prize money for the smallest of races can be only around £5,000, though, so an owner's percentage of a fourth prize totalling about £250 is not going to cover an awful lot. A slightly better race can be worth £10,000, with the best worth £100,000 or more. Prize money is usually a little lower in jumping than the Flat.

It is a frequently quoted fact that the average British owner recoups just 26p of every £1 spent on having a horse and average prize money is markedly lower than in countries such as France and Australia. As said before, it's a leisure activity, and British racing still offers as enjoyable an experience as anywhere. Racing executives are concerned about prize money levels, and are attempting to shore up ways that possible revenue can escape through the likes of betting and media rights.

Prize money is made up from a combination of streams. The biggest chunk comes from the government's levy of bookmakers' profits, and then in reasonably equal parts from the racecourse itself, the entry fees from owners and the race sponsors. Trainers want to run at the courses that offer the best prize money, so it is up to the tracks to attract sponsors and put money in themselves if they want to attract good fields.

It is possible to sponsor a race yourself, and many do. It is not just companies looking for some exposure in newspapers and television, either. Some great enthusiasts mark birthdays or wedding anniversaries by naming a race in their honour. Expect to have to pay about 20% of the prize-money fund, but this is often negotiable. Racecourses are always looking for new sponsors and will probably come to an arrangement involving a corporate box for the afternoon or evening.

▼ **There are sometimes grand trophies as well as prize money for big races** (*Keeneland photo*)

Types of ownership

Plenty of people are sole owners of one or many horses, having the right to register and choose their own colours and an input in decision-making. This power, of course, comes with the downside of having to cover all of the expense. Happily, there are a few entry levels, depending on cost.

The BHA has been running a scheme called 'in the paddock' referring potential recruits to a list of approved ownership groups with the aim of making the price and rules a little more transparent. They have a breakdown of rough costs, size and location, in order to find the best fit. Many trainers will also have shared ownerships or syndicate options available, or can suggest one to join if you contact their office. Do just remember, as with making any sort of financial investment, to seek transparency and paperwork in terms of costs and liabilities before you sign anything. And, of course, as with gambling or buying shares, your money is at risk of going down in value as well as, hopefully, up.

Join a racing club

The simplest way to start, a club is where you pay a membership for the experience of being an owner of one or a number of horses, but do not actually own the horse yourself. It is essentially more to have an interest and horses to follow.

By far the best-known of its kind in Britain is the Elite Racing Club, which costs £200 per year to join, has thousands of members and usually has more than a dozen largely Flat horses but sometimes jumpers trained around the country for them to follow. The Racecourse Association runs the Racegoers Club, which calls itself the sport's official supporters' club. Along with a basic membership fee as a starter, it has a small ownership scheme.

Most of the main clubs offer plenty in terms of newsletters, discounts, the opportunity to join visits to the stables and entry to a ballot for badges when a horse runs – there are often far

more people who want to go than the dozen or so that are usually allotted to enter the hallowed grounds of the paddock and the owners' and trainers' bar. Some clubs offer the promise of a share of any prize money won, which will be mentioned under their terms and conditions. As the horse is not owned, any proceeds from its future sale are not likely to be shared but, as the membership fee is fixed, neither will there be any scary veterinary bills to worry about.

Join an owners' group

This is the most recent development in ownership and is a little more than being in a club, but not as much as the next step of joining a syndicate. The group's manager will buy a horse, often one that will cost high five or even six figures, and have it trained by a top trainer. They will then attempt to sell a huge amount of shares for a one-off payment of roughly £50 each, with an individual shareholder then owning a minute percentage of the horse, perhaps 1/20th of 1%. They are then entitled to the same proportion of prize money and resale. It is much like a club, in that it is low-cost and low-risk, and mainly just to provide an interest in a horse, but with that small possibility of getting something back.

Join a syndicate

Being part of a syndicate is, to use a common racing phrase, to quite literally own the leg of a horse. Each has to have one responsible party, referred to technically as a 'syndicator' and at least two members, although syndicates can obviously range greatly in terms of size.

Syndicates are expected to become increasingly popular over the next few years as racing works harder to attract new blood. They have been restricted by extensive paperwork and red tape, but many authorities have noted the example of Australia where a simpler structure has seen the number of syndicates booming, and are following that example.

The easiest types to join as a starter are the large syndicates, just to get something of a feel for ownership. If not boasting a whole office of staff, they are usually run by a racing manager, who is the point of contact for members. In most cases, members must pay for a share of the horse when it has been bought and then a fixed monthly or annual payment, which will include training and bills as well as a management fee for running the syndicate. Depending on the agreement, there could be a return on prize money and resale of the horse.

Syndicates can start at a lowish price, a few hundred pounds for a percentage of the horse, and then a few hundred more for all of the training and running fees. At the top of the scale for many years in Britain has been Highclere Thoroughbred Racing, a syndicate with high-society

▲ There can be a lively social scene when involved in a racehorse

connections. Its joint-founder Harry Herbert's family seat, Highclere Castle, was used as the set for the popular *Downton Abbey* television series.

Highclere is not cheap – it could be around £10,000 for a 5% share including the purchase – and a smaller fee the next year. Its most exclusive syndicates cost at least as much as an ordinary horse on its own. However, it hangs its hat on being a more affordable way of being involved with genuine Classic-type Flat horses and the best trainers, as well as upmarket social events.

LEASING A HORSE

Horse breeders sometimes want to keep hold of a horse, especially if it is a filly and has possible breeding potential itself, but do not want to pay to put it in training. They will usually approach a trainer and ask them if they can find a syndicate or sole owner that will take the horse on and cover all of the training and racing fees for a year. While the owners have a horse they can race for an agreed time, they will not have to buy it, and keep all of the prize money accrued. After that stage, the horse returns to the breeder. The only real risk the temporary owners are taking is that if the horse turns out to be a good one, they may wish that they could keep it. It is very important to have fees, bills, duration and opt-out clauses all agreed in writing.

The role of a racing manager

▲ Racing manager Dan Abraham (centre, pink jersey) and members of his Foxtrot Racing syndicate at Cheltenham

In addition to being an elected chairman of the Racehorse Syndicates Association, Dan Abraham has around 160 members in his Foxtrot Racing business, with a number of different Flat and jump horses trained around the country:

"During a year when we had an average of ten horses, I sent 670 emails on to my members, which is quite a lot of emails when you think about it. It gives an idea of how much information I am trying to pass on, including every time the horse is entered, declared for a race, and how it's working. It's important to keep the members updated at least once a week, even if the horse is doing very little.

What it is about is making them feel like they are the sole owner, giving them that ownership experience despite the fact that they are not paying anywhere near the amount they would to have the horse on their own.

I probably spend 90 days a year going racing or to stables. I speak to the trainers regularly and make sure I'm going racing

when the members are, organise visits to the stables and also try to offer the additional value of being in a syndicate, so we have a party every October and organise an annual trip abroad going racing somewhere.

Not all my owners have been with me for ages and the majority of people that join are either having their first ownership experience or have left other syndicates and want a change.

I don't spend any money on advertising. It is all pretty much through word of mouth and recommendations by existing shareholders. I generally find that people in my syndicates know other people in their social circles who would fit in well.

Most of them are 20-person syndicates. The owner first needs the capital to buy the horse but after that it works out at about £1,300 per year. I think that's a pretty good amount, it's affordable for a lot of people and maybe similar to something like a good golf club membership, something people can compare with other things that they do.

I try to be very transparent. I produce final statements at the end of the year so they can see exactly what has been spent. What isn't spent, they get back, just as it would be with a sole owner."

Famous owners

Her Majesty The Queen

The Royal racing colours of purple jacket with gold braid, scarlet sleeves and black hat with a gold tassel are the most famous ones seen on a racecourse, tracing back from King Edward VII through King George VI to Elizabeth II. The Queen's fascination with racing developed in her childhood – her mother was a prominent jumps owner – and she became not only the first reigning monarch to become champion owner (twice in the 1950s), but more than half a century later the first to win the Gold Cup at Royal Ascot with Estimate in 2013. An active Royal interest has been taken in not only numerous horses running in Britain but even in Australia, as well as many more bred at The Royal Stud at Sandringham.

▶ Her Majesty The Queen

▼ The Queen's horse, Barbers Shop

▲ Sir Alex Ferguson has long enjoyed owning horses

Sir Alex Ferguson

In his time as Manchester United manager, Sir Alex Ferguson would use racing as a form of relaxation, with lots of his own good jumpers and Flat horses carrying his red and white colours, as well as others owned in partnership with friends. Ownership of his best horse, Rock Of Gibraltar, ended in acrimony. The colt, who he was involved with along with John Magnier's Irish Coolmore partnership, won seven consecutive Group One races including the 2000 Guineas, but the group fell out when Sir Alex was not included in the rights to Rock Of Gibraltar as a stallion.

Sheikh Mohammed

The man who was to become the Prime Minister and Vice President of the UAE and ruler of Dubai first went to the races at Newmarket in 1967 when studying in Cambridge. Ten years later, at Brighton, he owned the first of what became thousands of winners worldwide and the development of an operation that became hugely beneficial to the sport in Britain.

Interested in riding and horses since he was a child, Sheikh Mohammed now has breeding and training operations in Japan, Australia, America and across Europe and has won most

worldwide races of note running under the name of Godolphin, the ancient Arabian horse. He is a regular sight in Britain and has also invested heavily in creating racecourses and an entire racing community in his homeland.

The Aga Khan

Several generations of the Aga Khan, the title given to the spiritual leader of Ismaili Muslims, have taken a close interest in European racing for more than a century. The present fourth Aga Khan has stud farms in France and Ireland, which is where all of his horses are trained. His green silks with a red epaulette were involved in one of the sport's most famous tales when his colt, Shergar, who won the 1981 Derby by a record margin, was kidnapped when at stud in Ireland. Shergar was never seen nor heard of again in what still remains a mystery, with suspicion often directed towards the Provisional Irish Republican Army.

JP McManus

The green and gold-hooped silks of JP McManus have been seen on an almost daily basis in British and Irish jump racing since the 1990s. Born in Limerick in 1951, the Irishman first gained a reputation as a bookmaker and then as a seemingly fearless gambler, earning the nickname of 'The Sundance Kid'. McManus has owned some fabled horses, such as three-time Champion Hurdle winner Istabraq, with hundreds of others divided between many different trainers. A noted hurling enthusiast, McManus earned the rest of his fortune in finance. Many horses have seen out their days at his stud in County Limerick, while the man himself divides the rest of his time between London, Barbados and Switzerland.

◄ Sheikh Mohammed of Dubai is a regular sight at the sales and the racecourses in Europe *(Tattersalls)*

▼ The red silks of Sir Alex Ferguson alongside the green and gold of leading jumps owner JP McManus

What kind of horse to own

▲ Horses are shown off to active and potential owners at a stable open day

When becoming a member of a syndicate, there might be a choice of horses to have an involvement with. When buying one as an individual, it is a blank canvas.

The first decision to make is Flat or jumps. Most racegoers have an instinctive favourite, even if they enjoy both spheres of the sport. In becoming a Flat owner, the returns should be more immediate, particularly with a horse that has been bred to run quickly, and you might get the chance to see it race sooner than you think. Jumping can require more patience, waiting for conditions to come right for a horse that requires a particular type of ground to excel, and dealing with more frequent injuries. For many, though, having an interest in a jumper makes those dark winters more bearable and, injuries aside, you might get to see your horse race for several years more than if it was on the Flat. Picking a horse from a line-up, especially when it has not raced before, is pot luck without a wealth of expertise in physique and breeding but the most important thing for someone getting into ownership is simply that they find a healthy horse that should be able to race.

A horse can be bought privately from a breeder, via an agent, from an auction, or even from a selling race. It is a complicated process for a newcomer. Most trainers do buy some horses speculatively and advertise their wares in the media in order to find owners for them. They welcome enquiries and can usually find a type to suit needs and budget. Flat horses that have not raced are usually bought as one-year-old 'yearlings', while jump horses are slower burners and more available at three and four years of age. Horses can, of course, be bought as foals too, but will then need to go somewhere to be looked after before they can be sent to a trainer.

There might also be the decision between a colt or gelding, or a filly. Males are broadly more expensive because they win most of the major races and are considered easier to train as a rule. They also have a more tangible ability to earn rather than cost money if they go on to have a stud career. This is not to degrade fillies, most of which are very willing, and could also have a residual breeding value. Owning jumping-bred fillies was not popular for a long period, but there are now many more specific races for them and bargains can be found.

MEASURING A HORSE

The size of a horse is still, quite curiously, recorded in the anachronistic-sounding hands.

This measurement, the breadth of a human hand, was standardised as four inches by King Henry VIII in 1541. The size is its height, from the ground up to the top of the withers, or shoulder blade.

Thoroughbred horses usually range from between 15 and 17 hands.

▼ The height of a horse can vary wildly *(Keeneland Photo)*

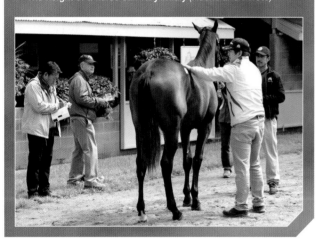

▼ There is no end of choice when it comes to choosing a horse *(Keeneland Photo)*

General types of horses to own

Horses are essentially grouped by cost according to their previous form, whether they have raced before and by their breeding, which can fluctuate according to fashion. They cannot exactly be categorised accurately, but below is a rough attempt to do so.

Fun horse (Flat)

Some owners have limited patience and want to see their horse running sooner rather than later. A more precocious type, or 'racy' in bloodstock-speak, is more suitable. These are cheaper and can often be purchased for a low five-figure or even a four-figure sum. These types of horses are often smaller and wirier, can be trained quickly and, provided there are no setbacks, can be ready to go as early as two years old. Be aware, though, that their most productive time is likely to be in the early days and they are unlikely to end up regularly running in good races over the subsequent seasons.

Backward horse (Flat)

Backward does not describe the direction in which the horse will necessarily travel, but more the idea that they will need more time to develop. Often, but not exclusively, these are horses that are bred to run over longer distances, they could be gangly and immature when they arrive and might not be ready to make their debut until they are three years old. The plus side is that they should continue to improve as they strengthen and can provide many years of enjoyment.

Classic horse (Flat)

You get what you pay for in horses, as in everything, and history has confirmed that only those bred to win Classics and other lucrative Flat races will end up doing so. Their fathers will have won Classics or other major races – and sometimes their

▲ The best-bred horses can cost considerable sums *(Tattersalls)*

mothers too – or they will at least be closely related to others that did. The best specimens will have the good looks and physique to match, but can command a six, or occasionally even a seven-figure sum.

Store horse (jumps)

The ultimate in long-term projects, these horses are specifically bred from jumping families and are often just living out in a field until they are three or four years old. They should be ready to be running at five and will hopefully have plenty of active seasons. However, they often need to steadily rise through the ranks and patience is required.

Point-to-point horse (jumps)

Some jump-bred horses have got their careers under way in point-to-points and are for sale as prospects that are ready to run in bumpers or hurdle races before graduating to steeplechases. It is not always easy to work out the merits of their performances in point-to-points, as they will have been racing against other unknown quantities. However, they have at least proved they have some ability and the most promising, sold at auction, will fetch sums equivalent to expensive Flat racers.

French-bred (jumps)

Horses start their jumping careers earlier in France and many are hurdling at three and jumping fences by four. Many of them are available for sale, with a healthy market from Britain and Ireland to buy them, as they are ready-made runners. For a long time, French-breds were considered to have a shorter career span than British or Irish-bred jumpers, but this has gradually become less of a stereotype.

Horses in training (Flat and jumps)

There are a few events each year where horses that have already raced go through the auction ring. Owners could have many different reasons to sell; they could have financial issues or want to make a profit on a horse that could command a good price. It is fairly plain that many are parting ways because the horse has not lived up to expectations, but this does not mean it should be the end of the road. Given a break and time to adapt to new scenery, a different training regime can rejuvenate a horse. Flat horses that have shown some stamina in the past can also make the transition to jump racing. Some real bargains can be found at this equine second-hand shop and many trainers are proud of earning a reputation for improving the cast-offs of others.

▼ Buying a horse already in training can be one way to pick up a bargain *(Tattersalls)*

In the past, owning a horse has been a laborious process in Britain, with antiquated procedures and reams of forms to fill out and return, either as a sole owner or as a 'partnership' of two or more with friends and family. Thankfully, the BHA and Weatherbys have been working on speeding things up and moving to the bright new world of technology. The traditional paper and pen method can still be used, by contacting Weatherbys for the forms. Horse Racing Ireland is also attempting to streamline its process and offers plenty of advice to owners, but there are still similar forms to be completed. The BHA has been helpful in providing the outline for the checklist below.

1. Registering as an owner

Any individual owner, or owner though a company or partnership, must register their details with the BHA. So too must those who want to run a syndicate or a racing club. Members of them do not need to. This costs £80 for an individual, and several hundred for setting up clubs, partnerships and syndicates. The BHA will need to carry out some checks to ensure you are a 'suitable' person, but this should only take a couple of working days.

Once registered, you have access to the Racing Admin website, which is where your horse can be entered in to a race. You will then be asked to register 'an authority' to act on your behalf – a licensed trainer – to make entries and add the horse into your ownership.

Do make sure you think about the name you use, as it will appear on racecards. A few years ago, three friends bought a horse without telling their 'significant others' and decided to call their venture the False Noses 'N' Glasses Partnership. The horse, Ted Spread, became high profile enough to run in the Doncaster St Leger, so they hardly got away with it.

2. Registering your colours

Once a registered owner, you will need some colours for your jockey's outfit. It costs around £50 per year to keep the colours, which can be chosen through the BHA. Racing silks originally derive from heraldic designs and many countries are liberal about the patterns and symbols that can be used

In Britain, there are 18 base colours to choose from and 25 different patterns on the body – 12 for the sleeve and 10 for the

PERMITTED SILK DESIGNS

Permitted colours
Beige, black, brown, dark blue, dark green, emerald green, grey, light blue, light green, maroon, mauve, orange, pink, purple, red, royal blue, white, yellow.

Permitted body patterns
Plain, seams, epaulettes, stripe, stripes, braces, hoop, hoops, quartered, crossbelts, chevron, chevrons, check, diamond, diamonds, triple diamond, spots, large spots, stars, Cross of Lorraine, star, disc, inverted triangle, diabolo, hollow box.

Permitted sleeves
Plain, armlet, hooped, striped, chevrons, seams, stars, spots, halves, diabolo, diamonds, check.

Permitted caps
Plain, hooped, striped, check, spots, quartered, star, stars, diamond, diamonds.

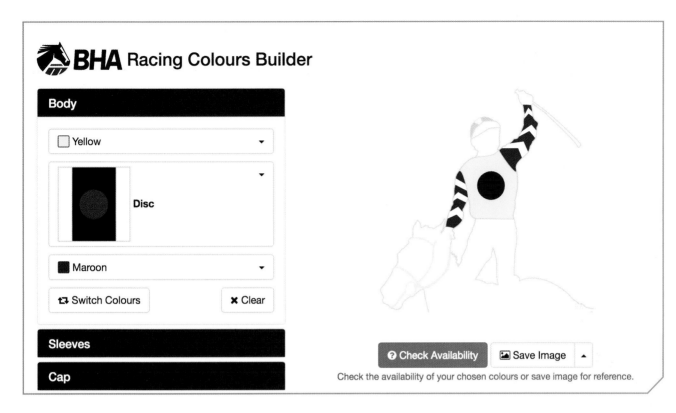

▲ A variety of colours can be chosen for your silks using the BHA colour builder *(British Horseracing Authority)*

cap – while very similar rules are applied to designs in Ireland. Obviously, many of these will have been already reserved, so it could be a matter of trial and error.

Most of the plainest designs have been in the possession of aristocratic families for generations, and still include tartans, braids and tassels, as well as colours not falling within the 18 approved base colours. They occasionally come up for sale at racing auctions, along with BHA-sanctioned classic and new designs and different plain-coloured silks, but all of these command huge sums and are usually picked up by powerful owners. The BHA does offer the opportunity to send bespoke designs to them, which will be considered for use, priced at £5,000.

3. Buying the silks

Once the colours have been registered, it is the responsibility of the owner to get them made. They can then be given to the trainer to look after. Smaller owners will only need one set, but the top owners, with horses in different stables and possibly runners at different tracks on the same day, are going to need to order in bulk.

It costs about £130 plus VAT and delivery charges to get your coloured shirt and cap, which can be ordered from several long-standing specialists. Allertons, a family business just outside Bicester in Oxfordshire, is probably the largest

manufacturer in Europe and proudly promotes its products as a 'hand-crafted, loving-care operation', all made on site.

Colours are not made of silk any more, but of a silk-feel polyester, weighing just 150g, with elastic cuffs and poppers down the front. They are cut out and sewn individually

▼ Colours are usually kept at the stable where the horse is trained

according to the BHA-approved designs. Allertons makes two sizes, with Flat jockey colours made to around a 36in chest and a jump jockey to 40in. They can also be made of an alternative weatherproof nylon fabric, so that riders will not be soaked to the bone in the middle of winter.

Just as fashions change in football and tennis, so it has been in racing. For some years, although not more recently according to an employee of Allertons, the use of tighter, lycra jackets became popular. As in cycling, the idea was to make a jockey more aerodynamic by reducing the drag co-efficient.

One of the trickier assignments for Allertons was to construct the colours for the Magnolia Cup. This ladies' charity race at Glorious Goodwood, which has featured former Radio 1 DJ Sara Cox in the past, has riders wearing one-off creations by designers including Jasmine Guinness.

4. Getting a training agreement

It is important to discuss and have an agreement with the trainer as to what you are likely to be paying. This includes the basic training fee and other likely expenses, such as if the trainer has to pay fees to use a public gallop and the cost of farriers. You should agree on the time and way to pay, as well as understanding additional charges including veterinary fees and travel costs. The Racehorse Owners Association and National Trainers' Federation have a template agreement that can be used.

5. Choosing a name

When buying a new horse, one of the most exciting parts is thinking of a name. There are, of course rules to it.

With what Weatherbys estimates to be around 250,000 names on the current register, many have been taken, but you can try anything in the BHA's search engine to make sure it is not reserved. It will then have to be approved to ensure no one is attempting to pull a fast one. Famously, Hoof Hearted was one that managed to slip through the net.

Approximately 3,000 names, usually of celebrated horses, are protected and cannot be reused, and suggestions can be

A NAME MUST NOT BE:

- More than 18 characters, including signs and spaces.
- More than seven syllables.
- Made up entirely of initials or punctuation.
- Start with a sign that is not a letter.
- Be in any way offensive.
- A name of a famous person or commercial entity, without gaining permission from them.

FIVE FUNNY NAMES

Owners and breeders amuse themselves by finding amusing names using the parentage of the horse, as well as being just plain silly!

- **Aironageestring** (whose father was Bach)
- **Safety Check** (whose mother was Doors To Manual)
- **The Gatting Ball** (for the cricket fans – his father was Hard Spun, and mother was Art Of Deception)
- **Court Drinking** (whose father was Alke and mother was Royal Forum)
- **Xilobs God** (best read the other way around!)

◄ **Many horses are given witty names, such as the self-explanatory Miss Inga Sock**

vetoed if they are too similar. Names of existing and not-to-be-protected horses do get freed up. It costs around £80 to register the name, more if it needs to be fast-tracked in a hurry. A name cannot be changed if it has already raced or bred any progeny in Britain or Ireland. Switching the name of a horse is considered to be unlucky anyway.

Other things to remember as an owner

Insurance

Horses can be insured against death, theft and to cover expensive emergency surgery through a number of professional organisations. It is not cheap – approximately 10% of the value of the horse – so it is more important for sole owners of a valuable asset. Syndicates often decide against

▼ **Most stables have sponsorship deals, which can directly help an owner**

this type of insurance to keep the cost down, and because their members will not feel the financial loss so deeply. It is a matter of choice.

Sponsorship

Most stables are sponsored by a business, which usually means the logo is on the horse's rugs, the stable staff's clothes and on the collar or the chest of the silks. Agreeing to this means your ownership counts as a business activity by HMRC and you are eligible to reclaim some of the VAT for expenses such as the purchase price of the horse and many of the expenses incurred. This can also apply to those involved with syndicates or clubs. Weatherbys provides several forms that are required by the tax authorities.

Sign a non-racing agreement

Unless you are able to keep a horse at the end of its career, it can be sold on to continue to do something else. A form provided by the BHA ensures it is prevented from reappearing again in races under someone else's name.

The breeding

From the vast, immaculately fenced and tree-lined studs in the racing heartlands of Newmarket and County Kildare to farmers who keep a mare in their field as a hobby, horses grow up in a variety of locations before we see them on the racecourse.

Breeding a horse can be as costly an investment as having one in training – and as much of a gamble. The farmer must choose a suitable partner (stallion) for their mare and then take her to the stud for the mating. There are plenty of complicated analytical tools and programmes to assess the genetics and best possible matches.

The mare will come back to the farm, eventually give birth and the foal will either be raised or sold. Over the following few months the foal could have growing problems and never make it to the racecourse, but if the mare gives birth to a horse that becomes a champion the farmer could soon be breeding other sisters and brothers that will suddenly command a far higher price if they choose to sell them. Buyers are most interested in young horses that come from successful families.

With other animals, and even different types of sporting horses, artificial insemination and even cloning are permitted. In the world of Thoroughbred

horse racing, however, a foal must be produced in the old-fashioned way. Only a few pre-eminent colts earn the chance of having a second career as a stallion, so the services and genes of the most successful come at a premium. Each encounter he has with a mare is euphemistically known as a 'cover'. According to 2016 figures, 4,663 Thoroughbred horses were born in Britain, where there were 155 stallions. There were 9,381 foals born in Ireland, which has 246 registered stallions.

This entire part of the process, from looking after the foal and those who work at studs to others that prepare horses for the sales and for their later training careers, is an almost separate industry in itself. There is so much international mixing of the Thoroughbred that close relatives of one horse could be racing on the other side of the world. News of successful offspring travels fast, and a youngster's value could double overnight if its brother or sister starts to show ability on the track.

The stallion

The sums involved with premier stallions are mind-boggling. Coolmore Stud in County Tipperary has become perhaps the most important such operation in the world, with a rolling cast of a couple of dozen Flat stallions spending periods both in Ireland and across continents, and incorporates a separate National Hunt division.

Coolmore developed the career of Derby winner Galileo, the champion sire for a decade whose covering fee was eventually listed as private, but was rumoured to have been raised to between €400,000 and €500,000. Sheer money, though, was not even the question, as very few owners would have a mare eligible enough to see him. Imagine then that Galileo could cover upwards of 150 mares in a season, perhaps for 15 years, and do the maths.

His son Frankel, the British superstar, had his fee set at

▼ **A Thoroughbred stallion is definitely the alpha-male of the breed**
(Irish National Stud)

▲ Tim Lane of the National Stud (right) offers some advice to bloodstock agent Jake Warren

£125,000 and there are other stallions that command high five-figure sums. They are, of course, extreme examples, and there are less fashionable stallions dotted around for just £1,000 or so, which do not see a high number of mares. The European covering season starts on 15 February, as many Flat horse breeders want to sell the offspring as yearlings. If the horse is bred earlier in the year, it will have the time to develop before the important races begin in the spring and summer. The big studs will start to close up by the end of June.

Rules in jump racing are looser. As male jumps horses are almost exclusively geldings, there are precious few stallions that ran over fences. Instead, jumping sires are primarily sourced from top-quality longer-distance Flat horses, which have more chance of passing on their stamina and durability. This is less so the case in France, where 'entire' horses are more frequently seen running over hurdles and fences and can eventually go to stud.

Jump horses are bred to start their careers as at least three years old, so there are fewer time pressures on when they need to be born. Jumping stallions do not tend to have high fees, perhaps because the breeder will need to spend more on raising the foals before they see any kind of return.

Alderbrook, the winner of the 1995 Champion Hurdle, is perhaps the best jumper of recent years to have become a stallion.

A day in the life of a stallion

The National Stud, just outside Newmarket, is a good place to learn about the breeding industry and has several active stallions during any one season. A business for more than 100 years, it was taken over by the Jockey Club in 2008. Not only can visitors book a tour year-round, it also holds a number of courses to earn qualifications in the industry.

Tim Lane, who manages the stud, explains how a stallion goes about his business:

His day will consist of being fed at 5.30am, then at 6.30am he would normally go on the walker for 40 minutes, or be walked, then go back to his box.

His first cover could be at 7.15am, and after the cover he would go back into his box or straight into the field, depending on if he had more covers. It all depends on if he has got a 12 o'clock, a four or an eight o'clock cover. If the weather is good, he could stay out all day.

Two or three days a week he would have a lunge. It's all about keeping him in order, healthy, happy and sane. Some of the stallions can be taken to Australia towards the end of the July, so they'll have a bit of a holiday outside and then go into quarantine.

Keeping the stallion mentally sound is the main thing. Some can get quite savage or difficult, and some will be Christians. Ours are very well managed by the team, but you do hear horror stories.

It's the testosterone, and they're territorial animals at the end of the day. In the wild they'd have a herd and they'd be the ruler of it. Some in training have bad temperaments, how they're bred can often relate to that, and when they come into the breeding shed it can be quite interesting.

The stallion can do four or five covers in a day if they are pressed for time – we try to leave four hours between each one – but it all comes down to libido and management.

The covering process

Breeding in horses has long been considered something of a secretive process, very rarely filmed, which usually takes place in a padded indoor arena known as a covering shed. For expensive Thoroughbreds, it is closely monitored by veterinary and equine experts and is anything but a romantic liaison between a boy and a girl.

As they are carrying out an important job, a stallion will have been given some 'match practice' with mares on the farm so that he knows what he is doing when so much money is at stake.

The National Stud's stud manager Tim Lane explains:

It's constructed sex really, it's all clinical and the mare, from a veterinary side, should be bang on for a cover. The stallion has got to come out of his box, come into the covering shed and do his job, but it's amazing the amount of stallions who, at the end of a long season, don't want to know. They just stand there and hours later you're there whistling at them.

It should be done and dusted in minutes. We 'bounce' all our mares, meaning that we have a male horse called a teaser, who we will bring in and present to the mare. He can jump up on her but has a bib on so he can't penetrate. Then the stallion will come straight in and hopefully get on with it straight away.

There will be four or five people in there at least – the stallion man, someone holding the mare, maybe someone holding her foal and someone who holds the tail and makes sure the stallion has ejaculated.

▼ A stallion takes a walk through the grounds of the Irish National Stud

The broodmare

A mare should usually earn the chance to become a mother if she is able to win a race or two on the track, as she has then proved her own physical capability and might be able to pass that on down the line. The pedigree is vital though; if a mare has been an ordinary racer or sometimes did not even run at all, she can still be bred from if she is related to other good horses. It is only amateur breeders producing horses from badly bred or badly put-together mares that pose a risk to the strength of the species as a whole.

A mare used for breeding, or a 'broodmare' lives on a stud or private farm, usually socially with other mothers and foals in tow. The gestation period in horses is around 11 months and so, with the idea that in the wild a foal would have a better chance of survival if born in the warmer spring and summer months, that is when a mare will come into her cycle.

A popular stallion will have a heavy schedule and breeders want their mare to be ready and receptive for their meeting, but veterinary improvements mean they can have a fair idea about timing. The weather can have a major impact and some farms will leave their lights on overnight around late December through January so mares at least start thinking spring is on the way. They might also be given certain feeds or supplements to help the libido.

Paying the stallion fee is subject to the mare falling pregnant, so if this does not happen first time, it is possible to bring them back for a second visit. The mare will then return to her normal life until ready to foal. There are different methods of detecting when a mare is about to go into labour, and some operations use various types of alarms or electronic detectors.

At the National Stud, there is a dedicated foaling unit. Tim Lane explains: 'Every box has a back door with a glass window and someone is checking frequently through the night. You'd hope you'd know – they start bagging up (the udder swells), they begin to wax, which is a secretion on the teats, and they can be a bit restless and might lie down or start sweating.'

▼ **Foals and their mothers are always closely monitored** (*Irish National Stud*)

Usually the mare can give birth by herself, but staff are on hand to help out, especially if legs are out of position or it is a big foal in a smaller mare. The foal should be on its feet and feeding quickly, and in the sad cases where a mare dies in delivery or the foal does not take to its mother, it can be found a foster mare.

Weakening of the breed

A problem with the Thoroughbred is the small gene pool. As mentioned already, the breed was founded on a handful of Arabian horses and in modern times, has been dominated by Northern Dancer and his sons and daughters.

This means that very few horses are not related to each other in some way or other and there are no laws against incestuous breeding in racehorses, even if a brother and a sister would certainly cause alarm. It is quite frequent to see a horse bred by a stallion and a mare that share the same great-grandfather, and it's pretty hard to avoid close relatives going further back. Oddly, it can still be desirable to have certain duplications at places in a family tree if this has been found to produce a high-class racehorse in the past.

Studying the pedigrees is quite a head-scratching job, and breeders use analysts to suggest suitable stallions that they should send their mares to in order to find the right formula. In recent years there seems to have been a growing desire for speedier and more precocious Flat horses that can win quickly and perhaps be sold on at a big profit to the very wealthy. The

▲ The global influence of pre-eminent stallion Northern Dancer has been passed on by his grandson Galileo and perhaps further by his offspring pictured here *(Tattersalls)*

biggest international races, the winners of which will become important stallions, are over a mile and a quarter rather than longer distances, and some of the more robust, later developing bloodlines fell out of fashion. These days, there are fewer of the patient owner-breeders who ran their operations with a view to future generations rather than cold-eyed business acumen.

Some two-year-olds have even been retired to stud after just one season. While they will have proved their ability, there is no time to have seen whether they would have either longevity or physical defects, which they could be passing on to their offspring. The breeding industry as a whole has been guilty of short-sightedness in this regard.

The narrowing of the gene pool also necessitates the importation and exportation of horses from overseas in order to provide more variety. Australian stallions, famed for their speed, have been popular in Europe, while more stamina-imbued stallions and mares have crossed the globe in the other direction. British and Irish markets have also looked to Germany and France in order to mix things up.

As the British and Irish blood is so highly prized, capable colts that might not quite have reached the standard to become a stallion on home shores can be exported to Asia or more minor European racing nations in order to improve their gene pool.

The foal

Growing up

Once the foal has been born (usually weighing around 125lb), it will spend five to six months with its mother, depending on its size and condition. This can include, should the mare's owner decide to breed from her again, a trip to another stud and a slightly disconcerting few minutes being held in the covering shed.

The hungriest and most curious can be known to start putting their heads in a manger after six weeks and eating 'grown up' food. They should not need milk from three months onwards and will enjoy a leisurely childhood out in a field with a few other mares and foals.

After this time, if the mare is pregnant again, she will need to concentrate on building up her strength, and the foal will be weaned (separated) from her. Foals are usually becoming quite independent by this stage anyway and are separated to live with a gang of other playmates. It is only by the time the foals are becoming yearlings that they need to be separated into groups of colts and fillies, to prevent any young teenage urges. They are usually kept with those of a similar age and size.

▲ A young foal might even find itself in the unfamiliar environment of the sales ring *(Tattersalls)*

▼ Youngsters have plenty of social life when growing up *(Irish National Stud)*

Sales preparation

If the foal is to be sold the following summer or autumn as a Flat yearling, or as a three- or four-year-old jump prospect, it will require a couple of months at the 'equine nursery school' of sales preparation. Either at the farm where it has grown up, or by being sent to a specialist business, the young horse will become more accustomed to its future life living in a stable.

Here, they will have initial handling, having bridles, rugs and head collars put on for the first time, and will build up muscle and strength by being walked by hand and lunged each day. Lunging is carried out in a circular enclosure. The horse is attached to a long rope, with a handler in the centre. The handler will manoeuvre the horse around in circles, starting to get it to turn left and right. The key aspect of this is to get it to listen to instructions. The horse will only do what it wants to do, so the experience has to be gentle.

In order to make it look more attractive to buyers, the staff will want it to walk well, behave properly, look healthy and be able to show itself off when it goes to the sales. Being more used to human interaction is also extremely important. Farriers have trimmed their feet as foals and yearlings, but this is usually the time they are fitted with shoes for the first time.

There is no set way to raise a racehorse, and those who teach yearlings these lessons adapt it to an individual's needs. A big, strong colt that is eating well will simply need more exercise than a fragile, pickier filly.

Going to a sale

Anyone can buy a horse, but not straight away. The sales company will ask you to register as a buyer first and make sure you are suitable to do business with. They will get hold of a bank reference and will either be happy to supply credit, or might ask for a deposit of around the amount you are thinking of spending.

Then you are ready to go. The horses are stabled in numbered barns on site before going into the ring so potential purchasers can inspect them. The grooms will walk them up and down, ask them to stand still, and some owners will ask their vet to give the horse a once-over. X-rays and other information on the horse can be viewed in the sales company's repository.

The bidding process is fairly similar to those for artwork or property, with the horse paraded around the sales ring, usually for several minutes, as the auctioneer tries to drum up interest and secret games of bluff take place. An interested bidder is advised to clearly indicate to the auctioneer for the first time, perhaps with a wave, then by adding another gesture if they want to bid again. Bid spotters scan the room, but buyers are advised to always bid to the auctioneer.

Unless a horse fails to meet its reserve, the hammer will come down and a ticket must be signed. Full payment is usually expected within a month. As soon as it has been bought, the auction house likes the horse to be moved fairly quickly, so a horse transporter must be enlisted. It immediately becomes the responsibility of the purchaser, or the transporter, to feed and water it. Many purchasers will request for the horse to be wind-tested, to make sure they are not buying a horse with potential respiratory issues.

There is no chance of a refund if the horse turns out to be useless, but there are possible reasons to bring it back if problems are not advertised. Animals exhibiting bad habits such as wind-sucking, box-walking and making whistling or roaring noises identifiable as breathing issues can be returned. Disputes and controversies do arise, with the occasional conman pulling the wool over a trainer or agent's eyes and attempting to defraud them, so the sales companies are always vigilant against unusual behaviour.

▲ **Tattersalls in Newmarket is the oldest bloodstock auctioneer in the world** *(Tattersalls)*

Tattersalls

Founded in 1766 and first situated right next to Hyde Park Corner in London, Tattersalls is the oldest bloodstock auctioneers in the world and probably still the most important. Its earliest sales were not just for racehorses – lots included horses for hunting and even pairs of dogs!

More than £250 million is turned over through the ring at Tattersalls' modern base in Newmarket, and its team of auctioneers and administrators are regularly required to preside over other sales in far-flung corners of the world. It has incorporated other sales at Ascot, Cheltenham and Fairyhouse in Ireland, offering approximately 13,000 horses a year.

At different times, it is possible to purchase foals and mares, jumps-bred older horses or horses in training, which have been with other owners and trainers. The serious money is for Flat-bred yearlings, and Britain's premier event is the October Yearling Sale, where countless young horses that go on to become winners of Classics or many important races are bought.

Anyone can attend a sale and the part containing the best-bred and likely most expensive yearlings, known as 'Book 1', is the most interesting for people-watching. Sheikhs from the Gulf and others of unimaginable wealth from Russia, America and the Far East will all be sizing up the equine talent. It is not unusual for the bidding to pass seven figures, and the ring descends to a hush as it becomes clear that several people are keen to have the same horse. This is, of course, a completely unproven horse and no one knows if it will be any good at all, yet sometimes Monopoly money is being spent on them purely out of ego.

Tattersalls still uses the old-fashioned guinea as currency, which equates to £1.05. As they are bought in guineas and sold in pounds, the difference between the two is where Tattersalls makes its profit. The firm's main rival is Irish firm Goffs, which also holds sales in Britain. As Flat racing is so international, yearling buyers will travel to Deauville in France, Baden-Baden in Germany and the likes of Keeneland in America for their sales through the autumn.

◀ **A busy session in the Tattersalls ring** *(Tattersalls)*

Buying a horse

Those with an equine background might have a fair idea of what a good horse looks like and may want to pick one themselves, but bloodstock agents are usually trusted by potential owners as they are more experienced judges of an animal's pedigree, physique, athleticism and any potential problems it could have.

Although ostensibly well-spoken gilet-wearing used car salespeople, most know what they are doing and understand the intricacies of the sales. There is a Federation of Bloodstock Agents to point in the direction of reputable individuals, but as with anything it is up to the buyer to decide if they like and trust them.

They make their money from commission and will usually ask for 5% of the sale price of the horse. This should be formalised before any bidding. It is a world that thrives on rumour and whispers, and the best-connected of agents know who is interested in which horse and have a good idea of how much they are likely to fetch in the ring.

The biggest money is for yearlings, but there are separate sales for different age groups and some for horses already in training, which just have to be entered and hopefully sold. For new horses, the price of the horse and where it came from

▲ **Agents, trainers and potential owners assess the potential of new young horses** *(Keeneland Photo)*

can have benefits. Some Flat races are restricted to horses that were bought at the lower end of the spectrum and some of the sales companies sponsor valuable races confined to their graduates. In jumping, many of the novice hurdles are for horses sired by specific National Hunt stallions rather than more Flat racing types, in order to keep those stallions relevant and desirable.

THE GREEN MONKEY

A sale of two-year-olds in Florida in early 2006 was the scene of an extraordinary bidding war. One young colt with seemingly perfect ancestry had run a very fast time in practice and two of the biggest players in the game wanted him. A battle developed between bloodstock agent John Ferguson, representing Dubai's Sheikh Mohammed, against Coolmore Stud's Irish buyer Demi O'Byrne. The two sides had been fierce rivals for many years. With neither agent wanting to back down, the final bid landed for O'Byrne for a world-record $16 million.

The colt was named The Green Monkey after a golf course in Barbados part-owned by the Coolmore partners John Magnier, Michael Tabor and Derrick Smith and sent to the leading American trainer Todd Pletcher. After some physical problems, The Green Monkey did not race until the following year, but failed to win in three starts and was ignominiously retired.

▲ The purchase of The Green Monkey was a very rare error by the Coolmore team, headed by John Magnier (centre in cap) *(Tattersalls)*

Studying the page

At each sale there is a thick catalogue and each horse, or 'lot' can be studied some time in advance, so the buyer can narrow down the ones they are interested in. A horse's pedigree is also known as its 'page', because each lot in the catalogue has a full page explaining its background. It is listed in far more detail than it would be on a racecard, including the horse's first dam (mother), second dam (grandmother) and third dam (great grandmother). It will usually list the achievements of each along with those of various siblings. Details are lighter on the sire (father), as most are well known and statistics on the records of their offspring are well covered in bloodstock publications.

When a horse has won or been placed in a Listed or a Group race, this will be written in bold in the catalogue. This is the reason you might hear the expression 'earning black type' when someone talks about a horse running well in a big race. The ability of the sire and the dam are both important in passing on their genes and there is often talk of a parent being good at leaving their mark (often described as their 'stamp') on their offspring. This is no guarantee on them being able to run fast, but it is a useful start. Those who pore over the information are

either looking for a particular type, be it a sprinter or a three-mile chaser, or simply the right kind of combination of blood that might be the recipe for a champion.

What to look for

'There are no such things as walking races' is a common refrain among those in the bloodstock world. However, the way a horse walks is considered about the most important thing to judge. A basic requirement is an 'overstep', meaning that the hind legs reach beyond the hoof prints made by the front legs. It shows that the horse uses itself well, and should translate to when it runs. A horse should move straight and fluidly, which is a rule applied to looking at them in the paddock before a race.

Experts will look at an animal from the side, front and back. They are checking that it is in proportion. Around the knees are of particular importance, as knees tilting backwards or forward, or 'offset' to the sides are negatives as the horse develops. The actual size of the heart and lungs cannot be measured, but buyers want to at least see evidence of a decent ribcage housing them.

For much of the rest, beauty is in the eye of the beholder. Essentially a horse should look in proportion and broadly symmetrical, with a strong neck. It also helps if it has some presence. A confident, bright-eyed, intelligent-looking horse,

◀ All of a horse's family details are listed in its 'page' in a sales catalogue. This beautifully bred colt turned out to be the future Derby winner called Australia *(Tattersalls)*

▼ Long ears are considered good signs of intelligence and honesty *(Tattersalls)*

compared with a timid or uninspiring one, is easy to spot, even for a novice.

Potential bidders are attempting to marry up the combination of the horse's athleticism with the potential in its page. The two together will make the eyes of its seller light up with pound signs. Even a horse with an ordinary pedigree can reach a good sum if it walks well, as some buyers will trust their eyes over what is down on the paper. But a well-bred horse with physical deficiencies will be less popular.

There are, of course, many 'old wives' tales' on the circuit. Long ears are considered a sign of honesty and a good nature, while chestnut mares are reputed to be bad-tempered. There are variations of a rhyme for when horses have white feet: 'One white leg, buy him. Two white legs, try him. Three white legs, send him far away. Four white legs, keep him not a day.' However, having four white legs did not seem to harm California Chrome, who became the leading money-earner in North America in 2016 with US $14,752,650.

Breeze-up sales

Two-year-old horses can be bought at an arranged 'breeze-up' sale before they have raced in public. Held early in the season on a racecourse, a young horse will be ridden solo in what is effectively a time trial. They are timed over two furlongs, when being asked to gallop to full effect by their jockeys, and then sold at auction.

Buyers are also scrutinising the horse's pedigree and physique, but a fast time proves ability and the quickest will fly through the ring too, as this is the nearest thing you will find to a horse that is a potential winner ready to race in the near future. Breeze-ups are a particular domain of what are known as 'pinhookers'. These are people who buy horses as yearlings and then prepare them to do well at a breeze-up sale with the idea of turning a good profit on them. Pinhooking can also apply to buying a foal and reselling it as a yearling in a normal sale. They can either work for themselves or for partnerships and investors.

▲ California Chrome, apparently 'unlucky' with his four white feet, was good enough to become the leading money-earning horse of all time with his win in the Dubai World Cup *(Andrew Watkins/Dubai Racing Club)*

For every spectacular success, there are obviously many failures with pinhooking. They are speculators, sometimes buying the offspring of a young and unproven stallion, trusting their judgement that the stallion will be more respected in a few months' time. This can obviously go the wrong way, and the individual horse they bought might not make the expected progress. Even the exchange rate can have a profound effect on the pinhooker's profit.

▼ Horses at a 'breeze-up' sale are ridden and timed in public *(Tattersalls)*

Breaking in

After a young horse has been sold, remember that it may not have even been ridden yet so it is far too soon to be sending it off to a trainer. It now needs to be 'broken in', so a jockey will be able to jump on its back and ride it. This tends to be done in breaking and pre-training yards, which are much like racing stables and not always a whole lot cheaper in terms of cost for their services.

The biggest mistake these practitioners can make is rushing the horse. Some will be happily cantering away with a rider in a matter of weeks; with others it is a long exercise in patience and building up trust. If the breaker is not familiar with the horse when it arrives, they will get it exercising on a long rein and lunge it around a ring before trying anything more complicated. Most follow a similar process, building up small changes over the days.

Its first big challenge is fitting the horse with a roller, which is a pad like a girth and straps around and under its stomach. The animal feels a weight on them for the first time, and will often have a bit of a buck and a kick. Side reins will then be attached, going from the bit to the roller. The idea is that the horse will start getting used to the feeling of the bit in their mouth, and having some contact with it.

Once it has walked around and been lunged wearing tack

▼ Young horses will not be ready for racing straight away

for a while, it is time to introduce a saddle and the sensation of stirrups clanking around by its stomach, followed later by more reins, teaching them to turn and respond to being moved left and right. Finally, it can be driven along by two reins, with a person walking along behind it. This is important for making sure the horse can stop when the reins are pulled.

As long as the horse's tutor is satisfied with its behaviour, the final procedure can take place for someone to get aboard. This must be taken especially steadily, with the rider usually jumping down quietly next to the horse before they are helped up and very gently lie on its back. The horse will be led around like this before the rider can start moving around on its back or touching the sides of the horse.

Finally, as using the legs is a vital means of encouragement, the rider will start to apply a little bit of pressure and slip their feet into the stirrups. In an ideal world, the horse will then happily allow itself to be ridden around the barn or ring where it has been broken in, and start trotting and learning to move in figure-of-eights, much like children practise on experienced riding school horses during their lessons. Horses are never going to be pushed by a breaker into running quickly, they just want it to learn some discipline and, as equestrian people tend to say, some 'manners'.

The remarkable American Monty Roberts has a quite different approach, using a technique he taught himself when having to round up wild mustangs for a rodeo. Often referred to as a 'horse whisperer', Roberts uses body language to offer kindness to a horse and is able to quickly build up a relationship with them. In a demonstration that he has shown around the world, he can get a horse to take a saddle, bridle and rider in 30 minutes.

Pre-training

Pre-training is often an extension of the breaking-in process. A horse goes through gentle cantering exercises before it joins its designated stable, depending upon the intensity of workouts suggested by its new trainer.

The horses can easily go to a stable and then back to a pre-training yard again if it has injuries, setbacks or just needs to be taken out of the training regime to grow and develop a little more. Often, racing stables have little space to turn a horse out into a field for a longer rest, or the time to dedicate to giving a recuperating horse a progressive exercise or walking programme to build it back up. The trainer has to focus their attention on managing the horses that are in a full work schedule, and will send some back to the pre-trainer with an agreed programme.

While some horses are at a pre-training yard to do some exercise, others visit just for a holiday out in a field. The fees the pre-trainer charges depend upon how much individual time their staff have to spend with a horse.

The future?

On the edge of Lambourn is a machine that, on first inspection, looks as if it might be part of an amusement park rather than anything to do with horses. In fact, it is a pre-training system that was decades in the planning and millions in the spending by its inventor, Mehmet Kurt. The Turkish industrialist and racehorse owner had begun to notice how many of his purchases were developing leg and muscle problems in pre-training and became convinced there was a solution.

He believed some of the effects were being caused by rider error and landed upon the concept of a machine that could do the preparatory work instead. Horses are loosely harnessed into a cabin that moves at a controlled speed from a walk up to 35mph around a six-furlong track, the idea being that they can move more naturally without the rider. Everything from their heart rate and lung capacity to the way they move is monitored and recorded. A human sits in the cabin and the machine cuts off if a horse stumbles.

Kurt built a prototype in Turkey but wanted his system to be showcased to the wider racing world and, being an Anglophile, chose Britain. It was eventually opened for public use in 2017.

▲ Turkish businessman Mehmet Kurt spent many years formulating his impressive machine *(Kurtsystems)*

▼ The Kurtsystem allows many horses to be pre-trained together *(Kurtsystems)*

Going racing

If not initiated into the game by their parents, most people's first experience of going racing will be when invited by friends or for a work function; so deciding when to go is not necessarily a decision one has to make oneself.

When picking, though, one is spoilt for choice. The busiest days are predictably on Saturdays or Sundays in most parts of the world, while there is usually at least one meeting in the south and north of Britain every day. Some in the evenings during the summer are combined with a post-racing concert. There are no less than 1500 to choose from, and races can be found on websites such as www.britishhorseracing.com.

RACECOURSE VENUES

Key

◆ Flat & National Hunt

◇ Flat

◆ National Hunt

○ All weather Flat & National Hunt

□ All weather

Perth Hunt
Hamilton
Ayr
Musselburgh
Kelso
Newcastle
Hexham
Carlisle   Sedgefield
Cartmel
Redcar
Catterick   Thirsk
Ripon   Beverley
Wetherby   York
Pontefract
Haydock   Doncaster
Aintree
Market Rasen
Chester   Uttoxeter   Southwell
Bangor
Wolverhampton   Leicester   Nottingham   Fakenham
Ludlow   Warwick   Yarmouth
Worcester   Huntingdon
Stratford   Towcester   Newmarket
Ffos Las   Hererford
Cheltenham   Windsor
Chepstow   Ascot   Chelmsford
Newbury   Kempton
Bath   Epsom
Wincanton   Sandown   Lingfield
Goodwood   Plumpton
Taunton   Salisbury   Brighton
Exeter   Fontwell
Newton Abbot

Down Royal
Sligo   Downpatrick
Ballinrobe   Roscommon   Dundalk
Navan   Bellewstown
Kilbeggan   Laytown
Galway   Naas   Fairyhouse
The Curragh   Dublin
Leopardstown
Limerick   Thurles   Punchestown
Gowran Park
Listowel   Tipperary   Wexford
Killarney   Clonmel   Waterford &
Cork   Tramore

Checklist for going racing

■ Look at the weather forecast. Remember that a large proportion of the day will be spent outside!

■ During poor winter weather, meetings can be abandoned. Racecourses provide updates on track inspections on their websites and via social media.

■ Have cash with you. Most racecourses have an ATM, but this is not guaranteed.

■ Check train times online. Some racecourses offer a complimentary or subsidised pick-up service from the nearest station.

■ Bring binoculars. There is usually a big TV screen to watch, but this can't always be found at small venues.

■ Carry a pen and notebook for noting down those all-important winners.

▲ A set of binoculars can help you follow the action from afar

Entrance

It should cost around £15 to attend a small midweek meeting, where a ticket normally allows you access to anywhere on the course. At bigger tracks, and at weekends, it's usually more like £25. A rule of thumb is that the smartest part of the track will be known as either the Premier or Members' enclosure. Here, facilities are usually better, there are nicer bars and restaurants, and the stands will be closer to the finishing line.

▼ **There is always plenty of colour on a day at the races**

The next best is often called the Tattersalls or Grandstand enclosure, where it's less formal but still easy to see the racing and to get something to eat and drink. At some racecourses, there will be an even cheaper area called the Silver Ring, or possibly a Family enclosure, usually an open space that is further away from the action but good value for money.

It is not necessary to book many days, apart from signature events – including the Cheltenham Festival and Royal Ascot – but it pays to check on a racecourse's website in advance, as there can be discounts for early purchases.

What to wear

Dressing for a day at the races depends upon the occasion. Most of the time in the winter, there is no dress code at all, as it is an outdoor sport and it's necessary to be prepared for the weather.

No one ever sticks out at a jumps meeting wearing tweed, especially at the Cheltenham Festival, which is a sea of brown and green hues. However, some of the more luridly coloured corduroy trousers that are teamed with sports jackets by regulars are a matter of personal choice. Hats are not necessary, although plenty go for a fedora or a trilby. Fur is fine but high heels are certainly not a good idea for purely practical reasons.

In the summer season, a good rule of thumb is to make an effort for a Saturday or a particular festival meeting, such as Chester or York. Midweek meetings are usually more relaxed and Sundays are often focussed on families so the dreaded phrase 'smart casual' is more appropriate.

A suit, dress, smart trousers or a jacket will do the job just fine at the weekend, as a bit of style never goes amiss. Smart denim is normally fine. The insistence that a tie is worn in the Members' enclosure is still the case at some of the grander racecourses, but this custom is gradually being relaxed. Still, it is usually better to be safe than sorry and to pull out all the style stops at a festival. Some showpiece meetings even have best-dressed competitions, offering cars, holidays and generous cash prizes. At Glorious Goodwood, in the middle of summer, the time-honoured look for men is a linen jacket and Panama hat.

A Members' enclosure will tend to make more of a fuss about ripped jeans, sportswear and trainers, while football shirts and bare chests will be frowned upon even in a Tattersalls

enclosure. Fancy dress (for stag and hen parties) is often allowed, providing the costumes are not offensive.

Dressing for Royal Ascot

The particular quirk of dress at the races comes at Royal Ascot, which has customs seen nowhere else. Having a ticket to the illustrious Royal Enclosure, which used to require signatures from other members but now simply requires an application form, means adhering to a very strict code.

▲ Hats are a must – the bigger, the better *(Shutterstock)*

▼ Tweed is always a smart option when going jumping at Cheltenham

▼ Panama hats are the form for a day at Glorious Goodwood

Dress code at Royal Ascot

Gentlemen

Black or grey morning dress including a waistcoat and tie (not a cravat), with a black or grey plain top hat and black shoes. The hat can only be removed in a restaurant, private boxes and facilities, and in outside seating areas in the garden. Overseas visitors may wear their formal national or service dress, while serving military personnel may wear their uniforms.

Ladies

Dresses and skirts that fall no higher than just above the knee, with straps and dresses on tops being at least one inch. Strapless, off the shoulder, halter-neck and spaghetti straps, or bare midriffs are not allowed. Trouser suits of matching material or jumpsuits can be worn, but they must be to the ankle. Hats must be worn, or a headpiece with a solid base of 4in (10cm) or more in diameter. Fascinators are not allowed.

The only other time such rules come into force is in the Queen's Stand at Epsom on Derby Day. Gentlemen will again need to be wearing a top hat and a black or grey morning suit or national/service costume, while ladies need to wear a formal dress or trouser suit with either a hat or a substantial fascinator.

For those not in the hallowed enclosures at these meetings, such strict rules do not need to be adhered to. However, this is a major social occasion and everyone will be dressed up to the nines. Beware: turning up in a morning suit at other non-Royal meetings at Ascot, or even on Oaks Day before the Derby, is considered a major faux pas.

▼ Access to the Royal Enclosure at Royal Ascot requires conforming to a strict dress code – even if you are a celebrity!

Parts of the racecourse

The stables and paddock

The runners for the day's races arrive by lorry a few hours in advance to settle in and have to go through a strict identification process of passport and microchip tests before being kept in one of the racecourse stables. These are well guarded and behind-the-scenes, as the safety and security of horses is vital.

The horses have to be formally declared an hour before their race and are brought through to a more public stable, where they will walk a few laps. A few minutes before the race starts,

they will be fitted with a saddle and bridle by their trainer and led into the paddock. The groom will walk their horse in circuits around the paddock, while the trainer, jockey and owners discuss race tactics.

This is the time for the public to take a look at the runners and assess their fitness and temperament. Once the jockey has been 'legged up' on top of the horse, it will walk around the paddock once more and then out onto the racecourse and let loose by the groom to head to the start at (hopefully) a gentle jog or canter.

In most racecourses, the winners' enclosure, where the first four in the race are taken back to, is in the paddock or a separate area nearby. The horses that finished outside the

▼ Final preparations take place at the racecourse stable

▲ A horse waits for race time in the stables

first few places are usually unsaddled on the track. There is time for the horses to have a drink of water and a hosing down back in the racecourse stables to cool off. They are led around until they have stopped blowing heavily and their heart rate has returned to normal, which can sometimes take at least 20 minutes. They are usually left for an hour or so to have a roll and relax a little before it is back on the lorry and off on the journey home. There are veterinarians on duty in case of any complications.

▼ A drink of water is needed to cool off afterwards

The racecourse

The joy of racing in Europe is the variety of its courses. Most are in an oval shape of between one and two miles, but they can be tight, wide or so undulating that the runners even disappear out of sight from the grandstands. At Fontwell in Sussex, the track is in a figure-of-eight while Newmarket, one of the world's most famous courses, is little more than a straight line. Some are multi-sport venues with golf courses in the middle, or even open farmland with sheep grazing.

A racecourse is far more than simply a large expanse of grass and maintaining it takes more work than might be imagined. The ground is maintained by a clerk of the course, assisted by a team of full-time staff who will irrigate, reseed, fertilise, spike and compact it through the year in order to meet with laid-out official guidelines.

Most tracks favour a blend of slow-maturing rye grass with robust roots and good ground cover, but types that do not need to be cut as regularly, given the expanse. The part of the track used for racing is surrounded by white running rails, which are now all made of easily bending interlocking plastic in case a horse runs into them. Manufactured largely by French company Fornells or Duralock in Britain, they are attached to the ground with metal spigots and are sometimes moved around in order for different parts of the surface to be used and to prevent too much wear and tear.

After each race, it is a regular sight to see a group treading

▲ Maintaining the ground and ensuring it is safe for horses is a big job

divots back into the track or conducting repairs on damaged fences. Distances of the course are measured in furlongs in Britain and Ireland (metres elsewhere) with large posts showing the number of furlongs remaining before the finish. There are often smaller markers dotted around, which could notify racecourse workers where the particular starting points are for races or to inform jockeys for where different parts of the track are being used.

The ground

This can vary hugely and is best described by Brian Clifford, the clerk of the course at Kempton Park racecourse near London, as imagining a walk on the beach. 'If you are standing by the water's edge, think of that as being firm,' he says. 'Then if you walk a few feet away, where the sand dries out, that's going to be soft, and good is somewhere in the middle of the two.'

Knowing the ground is vitally important when trying to work out the winner of a race because different horses perform better when it is firmer or softer. The clerk of the course will regularly assess the ground and provide official updates through the week using various measures. Most racecourses have sophisticated watering systems to ensure that the ground remains safe in dry periods.

When significant areas differ, ground can have variants such as Good to Soft (Good in places). In some countries, the word 'yielding' can be used to describe Good to Soft ground. Horses will only brush over a Firm surface but will plough right through Heavy ground, leaving their jockeys splattered with mud.

The ground is also officially measured by a contraption invented by a collaboration of racing experts, with the help of Cranfield University, called the 'GoingStick'. When put into the grass, it calculates the resistance of the surface and produces a digital figure between two, for very heavy, to fifteen, which is hard. A measure of eight would be the centre of good ground.

Turf ground descriptions

- ☐ Hard (rarely seen due to safety measures)
- ☐ Firm
- ☐ Good to Firm
- ☐ Good
- ☐ Good to Soft
- ☐ Soft
- ☐ Heavy

All-weather ground descriptions

- ☐ Fast
- ☐ Standard to Fast
- ☐ Standard
- ☐ Standard to Slow
- ☐ Slow

▼ The ground can be measured with a device known as a GoingStick

▲ **Even artificial surfaces need some maintenance**
(Keeneland Photo)

All-weather surfaces can also vary according to conditions but, in contrast to a grass surface getting slower to run through when it rains, they tend to speed up. It is generally accepted that a Polytrack races similarly to Good on grass, while Fibresand is more comparable with Soft.

Racecourses are at the mercy of the weather. Snow, frost and too much or too little rain can see a meeting abandoned for safety reasons. If a fixture is in jeopardy, news of a course inspection will be announced in the media, so it's worth checking before you leave.

Fences

Fences are positioned at intervals around a jumps track and there are three slightly different obstacles for horses to encounter in a steeplechase race. Officially there must be at least six fences for a horse to jump for every mile of an event. They are all at least 30 feet across and are usually built on-site with slim birch branches packed into a core made of wood and cut into shape. They are often slightly rounded-looking on the take-off side, marked by bright orange boards and padding so that riders can see them from a distance in gloomy conditions. Each fence, which is generally replaced every two years, is surrounded by plastic wings for extra safety.

▼ **A more detailed going description of Ascot racecourse**
(TurfTrax)

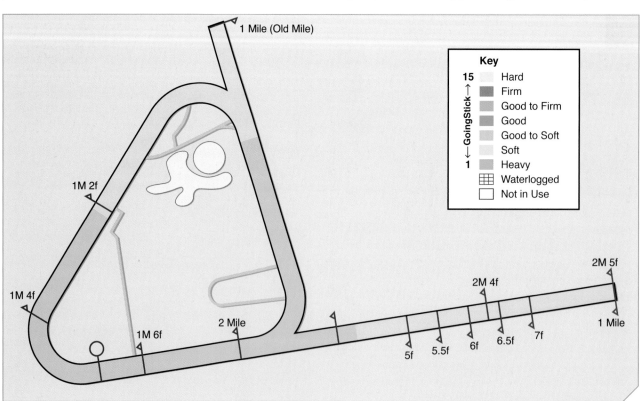

Types of fences

Plain fences

The majority of fences are known as 'plain fences', which are straightforward obstacles of a minimum 4ft 6in height, and 6ft to 6ft 6in depth.

Open ditches

There must be at least one 'open ditch' to jump per mile of a race. They are longer to jump, as they have a ditch on the take-off side, are of the same height but of 7ft 6in to 8ft depth.

Water jumps

Not every jumps course has a 'water jump', replicating the ditches full of water experienced when riding across open country, which are smaller in height than other fences but far longer and provide their own unique challenge to a race. In Britain they must be a minimum of 3ft height and 11.5ft to 12ft overall width, with the water being 3in deep.

▲ Clearing the water jump at Newbury

▼ Steeplechase fences are made from tightly packed birch

Grand National fences

The most famous fences in the world are unique to the Grand National course at Aintree near Liverpool. There are 16 of them, most of which are jumped twice in the marathon distance of the big race itself. All are green, as they are dressed with 150 tonnes of spruce transported from Grizedale Forest in the Lake District. The fences used to contain wooden posts but a 2013 safety review saw them replaced with a plastic core to make them more forgiving, and the landing sides were made more level. This has had a positive impact on horse welfare but has made it no less of a spectacle to watch.

The most difficult fences have become household names. The Chair, close to the stands, is the biggest obstacle at 5ft 2in and also the longest to jump, with a 6ft ditch on the take-off side. Becher's Brook has the most fearsome reputation. It is 5ft high with a steeper drop on the landing side, which mean riders must sit right back in the saddle in order to stay on board. Becher's Brook has been much refined since the eponymous Captain Martin Becher fell off in the first recognised running of the National in 1839 and hid in the ditch, waiting for the field to pass over.

Cross-country fences

Cross-country racing is a more obvious throwback to the hunting origins of jump racing, when all kinds of obstacles would be jumped. The discipline is more frequently seen across

▲ The green spruce fences of the Grand National are world-famous

France, while there is a famous course over banks and walls at Punchestown in Ireland.

There is only one cross-country course used in Britain, built in 1985 and winding around the inside of the other tracks at Cheltenham. It contains a variety of jumps, from hedges to grass banks. As there are only a few races a year, they do not have a particular following and many senior jockeys do not take part for fear of taking the wrong course and receiving a hefty suspension.

Nonetheless, many spectators like to take the opportunity of being allowed into the middle to watch the horses from a far closer vantage point than usual. Experienced and intelligent horses take to it best and can become regular and repeat winners. Risk Of Thunder, owned by actor Sean Connery, won Punchestown's signature La Touche Cup there an unprecedented seven times.

Hurdles

As hurdles are part of the education process for a horse, they are smaller and far more forgiving than fences, and at least four must be jumped for every mile of a race. They come in sections, driven into the ground on a stake, and are designed to collapse if a horse hits it hard. Each panel has a light timber frame and usually contains a slightly lighter brush birch than fences. The panels on the take-off side and the top of the hurdles are

▲ Cheltenham's cross-country fences offer a variety of challenges for horse and rider

protected with foam padding. They must be a minimum of 3ft 6in tall. In some of the lesser jump racing countries, what they would call fences are more like European-sized hurdles.

There have been a number of innovations with hurdles in recent years, with the trialling of plastic versions, and portable and 'fixed brush' hurdles, which are more like miniature fences, but there has not yet been an invention successful enough to initiate a national design change.

▲ Traditional hurdles are produced in sections and driven into the ground

▼ Fixed brush obstacles, such as these at Haydock, are more substantial than ordinary hurdles but smaller than steeplechase fences

▼ The hurdle panels fall down when hit by a horse

▲ Starting stalls give every runner the best chance of a level break

The start

Starting stalls (Flat racing)

Now one of the most familiar symbols of Flat racing, it seems strange that stalls were not even used in Britain until 1965. Before then, events were started in a similar manner to jump races today with runners lining up in a row, or even rows, behind a tape or barrier that would rise up and let the field go. This could lead to, at best, some disorganisation, and at worst, suggestions of favouritism and skulduggery, and a solution where every runner lines up level and is safer from bumping and interference had not yet been implemented.

Britain was far behind the times. An American, Clay Puett, had invented an electrical push-button gate that was first trialled in Canada in 1939, and by the end of the following year they were spread across the USA. They were also already being used in France before Lester Piggott won the first race using stalls at Newmarket.

Modern stalls are sent flat-packed from a company in Australia called Steriline. They are heavily padded on all of the panels in and around the individual compartments and have a spring-locked gate at the back, where the horses enter, in order to open them again quickly if an animal begins to get upset and needs to be released. Those that become difficult and unruly

during the important process before a race will often be ordered to report for an official stalls test on another occasion to prove they are suitable to compete.

The stalls are on wheels so that they can be towed off quickly if a race is over more than a lap of the course. Very occasionally there are malfunctions, with races declared void or individual horses counted as non-runners for betting purposes when gates have failed to open at the same time. In the case of serious stalls problems, races can be started by waving a flag instead.

In Britain, the Racetech company operates almost all of them. There are over 30 sets of stalls, ranging from 10 bays up to 17. Some courses own their stalls and others travel by road to different destinations.

Horse terminology

Colt	Male horse less than five years of age.
Filly	Female horse less than five years of age.
Mare	Female horse of five years and above.
Gelding	Male horse that has been castrated. Most male horses of five and above are geldings. If not, they are usually called either a 'horse' or an 'entire'.

The starting process

It is important for races to be started as close as possible to their scheduled time, which is where the experienced teams of stalls handlers come in. A staff leader and a minimum of ten other handlers, who invariably have a background with horses and have been formally trained and accredited, are on the ground to ensure the process continues without a hitch.

Horses leave the paddock and are ridden gently down to the start by their jockeys. They circle behind the stalls, where final checks and adjustments of their equipment take place, before the race starter orders the loading process to begin.

At some racecourses, it is possible to head down to the start to watch close at hand. Away from the crowds, it is a strangely peaceful time because jockeys and handlers have an agreement about remaining silent as the loading starts. Most horses become seasoned professionals and are familiar with what happens next. Six of the stalls handlers are there to lead the horse into the stalls and to duck down out of the front of the gates, and the other four are available to push them from behind if the horse does not go straight in.

Some horses can be far more highly strung and therefore difficult, which is why the handlers wear safety equipment. The first bit of coaxing is for another handler to start pushing from

▲ Well-trained stalls handlers lead every horse into the gate

▼ Some horses will cause more work for stalls handlers than others (*RaceTech*)

▼▼ The stalls handling team is a tight unit (*RaceTech*)

Monty Roberts rugs

One or two horses at the start might be spotted wearing a rather large blanket running from behind the saddle and around their back legs. These are for horses that suffer from an equine form of claustrophobia and get anxious when they feel the stalls on their sides. Named after the American horse behaviour expert, they are allowed, provided permission is asked for first and the blankets are automatically pulled off as the stalls open.

▼ A custom-made Monty Roberts rug is used on horses that have trouble with the stalls (*Gibson Saddlers*)

behind, using a woven piece of rope called a quoit. If this proves unsuccessful, the race starter will attempt to distract a horse by putting on a blindfold, which the jockey must remove before the stalls open. This often has the desired effect, but if not, the horse will be given one more chance once all of the others are in. If it still refuses to consent, it will be withdrawn. The starter gives the order, pushes the button and the race starts without it.

The practice is not uniform around the world. In America, there is room in each stall for a handler to stand inside to make sure each runner is under control. Horses are also all accompanied to the start by an outrider on a pony. They are herd creatures, so the idea is to help them relax, as well as being part of the tradition. Being a stalls handler is a dangerous job, especially when horses lash out, get upset or rear up in the stalls.

▼ Last-minute adjustments to the girth take place at the start

▲ Jockeys move into position for the start of a jump race

Tape start (jump racing)

There is less of a need to ensure the runners start in an exact straight line in jump races, none of which are less than two miles, given they do not set off at such a fierce gallop and many riders will want to use tactics from where they start at the rear of the field.

The responsibility for starting a jump race falls entirely down to a starter and his or her assistant. Once the horses have arrived and been checked over, they will walk in circles in a restricted area. At race time the starter raises their flag, which is an indication for jockeys to move their mounts into line and walk towards a tape that stretches across the track.

Provided the runners approach in a manner that the starter believes is safe and fair, they will drop the flag and release the tape at the same time. The start gets more complicated in the frenzied atmosphere of the Grand National, with 40 runners jostling for position. There have been examples when some runners have got too close to the tape, or even broken through it while other horses are facing in the wrong direction, leading to a false start being called.

The finish

The first horse to pass the post wins the race but it is the responsibility of the judge to confirm this. Since 1947, British racecourses have been operating with photo technology on the winning line, which comes in pretty useful when there is a

▲ Racing can be a sport of very fine margins

Official distances

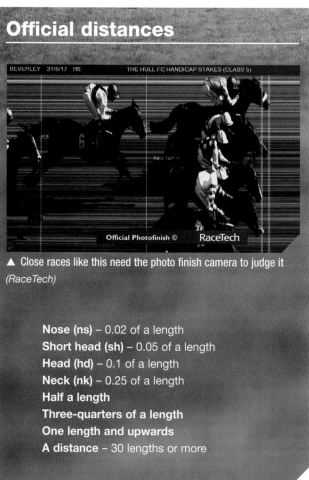

▲ Close races like this need the photo finish camera to judge it
(RaceTech)

Nose (ns) – 0.02 of a length
Short head (sh) – 0.05 of a length
Head (hd) – 0.1 of a length
Neck (nk) – 0.25 of a length
Half a length
Three-quarters of a length
One length and upwards
A distance – 30 lengths or more

tight finish. Thousands are riding on the result for those involved with a particular horse, and many millions when it comes to the global betting industry. After scrutinising the picture, the judge will announce the finishing order as well as working out the officially published distances between horses.

Distances are still referred to by the old-fashioned-sounding measurement of lengths – the length of a racehorse between its nose and its tail – or around 8ft (2.4m). The judge measures the distances based on the time elapsed between each horse on a

▼ RaceTech cameras even captured the Royal Procession at Ascot

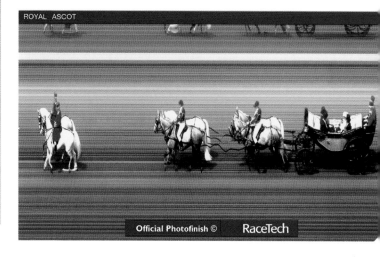

scale of lengths per second, which ranges between four and six depending on the surface and type of race.

If the two horses simply cannot be separated after extensive examination of the photo, a dead heat can be called. The first and second prizes will be split, while those who have had a bet on either horse get paid out, but only to half the stakes of their original bet.

The weighing room

Usually placed near to the winners' enclosure, this is the jockeys' inner sanctum where they prepare for a race. With races at half-hourly intervals, it can be a fleeting return for the most in-demand riders as they swap the colours that they are wearing. The complex usually consists of a room for the race stewards, changing rooms, a sauna and a canteen. The most important part, as suggested by the title, is where they are weighed.

Depending on what type of race they are running in, horses will have varying amounts of weight to carry. At least 15 minutes before the race is to begin, a jockey must 'weigh out'. This involves standing on the scales with the saddle in front of the officials and wearing their racing colours and boots. Safety equipment including the helmet and whip do not have to be declared, and neither does the number cloth, which sometimes contains a measuring device. Interestingly, the scale is set at -2lb rather than zero, to account for the body protector.

Should a jockey be lighter than the weight his horse is set to carry, the rest is made up using thin lead weights slipped into a cloth. The cloth and the saddle are then handed to the trainer or representative to be put onto the horse the jockey is about to ride. If they are above the weight, this will be announced, as it can have ramifications for the horse's chance of winning.

Modern jockeys do not quite resemble the Victorian stick-thin

▲ Jockeys undergo a strict 'weighing out' procedure before they can ride in every race (*www.focusonracing.com*)

cartoons but many will regularly have to sweat in order to shed a few pounds to make the correct weight for their horse. As people have become historically bigger, so the minimum riding weight has occasionally been raised. In 2013, it was brought up to 8st on the Flat in Britain (it is higher in most other countries), and 10st for jumping.

After a race, any jockeys who earned prize money (usually the first four) will have to stand on the scales to 'weigh in'. They are allowed to be a maximum of 2lb above or below what they weighed out at, to account for sweating or getting wet riding in the rain. There are serious penalties for greater disparities. The 'weighed in' announcement over the public address is the sign that the result is official and bets can be settled.

▼ Jockey Barry Geraghty leads Richard Johnson out of the weighing room at Cheltenham

Important racing bodies

Most of the significant racing countries have a national body that administers and regulates the sport. In Ireland it's The Turf Club and Horse Racing Ireland, and in France it's France-Galop. America and Australia have such matters divided into states. In Britain, a few organisations co-operate to organise, which is not always a smooth process.

British Horseracing Authority (BHA)

UK racing's governing body, based in London, became one such institution in 2007, and performs a number of different functions. The most obvious one would be enforcing rules. Through various departments, it looks after integrity matters, ensuring fair play and rooting out bad apples. Owners, trainers or jockeys guilty of corruption or misdemeanours (such as not trying to win) can be banned from attending racecourses or even stables for years if found guilty of serious offences.

When an incident happens in a race or on a racecourse that contravenes regulations it is first dealt with by the BHA's stewards at the track and serious matters can then be referred to headquarters. Should individuals choose to appeal, a disciplinary hearing will be organised in front of an independent panel.

The BHA is not simply racing's courtroom. It works closely with racecourses and participants, controlling the amount of

▼ The British Horseracing Authority's officials ensure the integrity and smooth running of the sport *(www.focusonracing.com)*

race meetings there are in Britain and what kind of races are at each meeting, in order to provide opportunities for every level of horse. It grants licences to trainers and jockeys, and monitors riders when they have suffered injuries.

As a governing body, it is also responsible for racing's funding, working closely with the government to ensure there are rules for contributions from bookmakers to pay for prize money, as well as training schemes and veterinary research. The BHA provides many of the people involved in the day-to-day running of racing, from the vets to the starters and judges, while its handicappers analyse every race and provide an official rating for every horse.

Weatherbys

This venerable institution, dating back to the middle of the 18th century, is racing's secretariat. It handles much of its administrative business, under contract from the BHA, from its office in Wellingborough in Northamptonshire.

Since the beginning of organised racing at around that time, James Weatherby's family firm has been the official keeper of the General Stud Book, which is a database of all Thoroughbred horses in Britain and Ireland. To this day, foals must all be registered with Weatherbys if they are going to be eligible to race. It also has a DNA testing lab in Ireland, which can determine parentage of horses and is also offered as a service for cattle and even domestic pets. Weatherbys can issue horse passports (as well as to ponies and donkeys) and keeps track of where horses are being trained, dealing with stable staff and their appropriate documentation.

It is also key when owning a racehorse, as it is responsible for registering the names of horses and the individual colours that the jockey will wear. It works with the BHA in taking entries for races and publishes and distributes the various data to the media. Other private services offered include pedigree analysis, with experts providing reports and statistics to breeders as they decide what sort of horses they want to produce.

Since its foundation, Weatherbys has also been a bank and provides many of the financial services for the sport, taking the various fees from owners and trainers as well as collection and payment of any prize money owed. It also has other private banking services, essentially dealing with high net-worth individuals, and not exclusively with involvement in racing, including the likes of mortgages, insurance and investment advice.

The Jockey Club

Once an organisation that fulfilled many of the duties now under the mandate of the BHA, The Jockey Club is the largest commercial group in British racing. A not-for-profit organisation governed by a Royal Charter, it owns 15 racecourses including many of the most recognisable ones, such as Cheltenham, Aintree, Sandown, Epsom and Newmarket.

The Jockey Club's land doesn't only include racecourses; the estate includes 2,500 acres of the Newmarket gallops. More recently it acquired 500 acres of training grounds in Lambourn, and is responsible for their upkeep and management. It has a private members' club on Newmarket High Street, the Jockey Club Rooms, featuring priceless artwork from the likes of George Stubbs and Alfred Munnings, and the preserved hoof of Eclipse, a legendary horse from the late 18th century.

The Racecourse Association (RCA)

The RCA is the trade association for nearly all of Britain's racecourses, promoting best practice, growing the sport and representing the interests of all the tracks, whether independent or as part of bigger groups, in industry discussion.

It also owns RaceTech, the company that has been responsible for providing photo-finish cameras, the majority of starting stalls teams across the county and the outside broadcasting of most race meetings. RaceTech's headquarters in Raynes Park, south-west London, therefore houses a remarkable archive of rare and old racing footage.

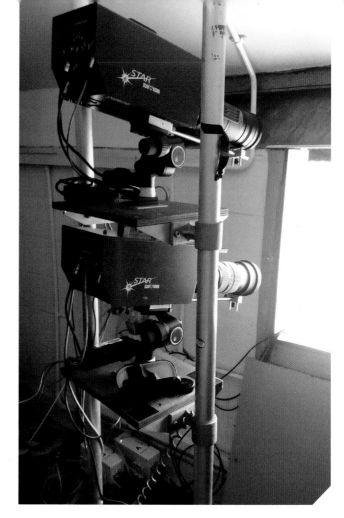

▲ RaceTech is responsible for the photo-finish cameras on many British racecourses (RaceTech)

▼ Cheltenham is one of fifteen racecourses owned by the Jockey Club

Types of races

There will usually be between six and eight races at a meeting in Europe, spread over half-hour intervals, divided into different grades and distances. Racing in Europe is less of a test of human stamina than in South America, where there can be as many as 20 races on the card!

Handicap

Every horse has a rating according to its ability, known as its 'handicap mark'. The horse carries weight according to that, so the better the horse the more weight it carries. Theoretically, all the runners should then finish close together. Handicaps are popular for betting, and is where most horses will end up; they make up approximately 60% of races run in Britain.

Group race (Graded race in jump racing)

The most valuable races for the very best horses, usually carrying equal weights. They rank from three up to one and include events such as the Cheltenham Gold Cup.

Classic races

The five historic and main Group One races for three-year-old Flat horses. They are the 1000 (females) and 2000 Guineas (males) at Newmarket, the Derby (males) and Oaks (females) at Epsom, and the St Leger (both) at Doncaster.

Listed race

A race for high-class horses that are just below Group level.

Conditions race

Usually for better-class horses with the weight carried dependent upon age or sex, while horses that have won before sometimes carry extra weight, known as a 'penalty'.

Novice race (jumps only)

A race especially for young horses. Horses are allowed to spend one year each as a novice hurdler and novice chaser in order to gain experience. If they do not win a race within this period, they can remain in this category until they do.

Maiden

A race for horses that have never won a race.

Bumper (jumps only)

Officially described as 'National Hunt Flat races', these are Flat races specifically for jump horses that have not run on the Flat, over hurdles or fences before. Usually over two miles, they are the first step of a jump horse's career before they start going over obstacles.

Nursery (Flat only)

A handicap for two-year-old horses.

Selling race (or seller)

A low-level race in which the winner is offered at an auction afterwards, while others in the race can sometimes be bought for a fixed sum. Should the representatives of the winning horse successfully bid for it themselves, conceding a percentage of the fee to the racecourse but having pocketed the prize money, the horse is announced as 'bought in'. A horse that regularly runs in such races is often known as a 'selling plater'.

Claiming race (or claimer)

Another low-level race, in which each horse taking part is for sale at a price fixed by its owner. The lower the price of the horse, the lower the weight they carry.

After the race

Every meeting is monitored by a set of stewards, to ensure the rules are being adhered to. Should they have any concerns into the running of the race, a 'stewards' inquiry' announcement will be broadcast. Usually a panel of three people, the stewards will watch replays of the race from different angles and call the jockeys in to their room, usually inside the weighing room, to offer their version of events. Applying the laws of an extensive rulebook, stewards have the power to disqualify horses from races. Issues that they might look into are as follows:

▲▼ Every race in Britain is closely monitored by BHA stewards and officials (www.focusonracing.com)

Interference

One of the most controversial occasions is when one horse has affected the chance of another by bumping, cutting across a rival, or by a jockey squeezing their mount through a gap that was not really wide enough to go through safely. The stewards must take into account where the incident happened, how well the horses were running at the time, how serious the interference was and how far apart the horses finished in the end before they make their judgement.

If the interference is adjudged to have improved the finishing position of the horse that caused it in relation to the one that suffered it, the positions can be altered. It is also permitted for jockeys to launch their own objection to a result if they feel they have been hard done by in the race.

Whether the interference was adjudged to be caused by dangerous, careless, improper or accidental riding does not predetermine whether the winner is demoted or disqualified, but it will impact upon how serious a penalty the jockey receives. This can range from a day's suspension from riding up to a whole month.

British and Irish stewards will tend to give the benefit of the doubt to the horse that finishes in front, and are generally considered more reluctant to change a result than those on the Continent. The further from the finish an incident happened, the less likely it is to affect the result.

Running and riding

All horses are required to run to the best of their ability and the jockey must be seen to be making a reasonable effort to win. Stewards are alive to the possibility that horses might not be 'trying', perhaps because the trainer or owner has another race in mind when there is a better chance it could win (as well as being longer odds in the betting), or for even more nefarious reasons. Jockeys are also required to keep encouraging the horse to finish in as high a place as possible, within the rules, and not settling for fourth place if they could easily have finished third.

There are serious ramifications for breaches of these rules, from four-figure fines to long suspensions. Should it be found that a jockey has deliberately ridden a horse to lose, or been instructed to – particularly if those involved have gained

financially from doing so – the perpetrators can be disqualified from having anything to do with racing for many years.

Jockeys will be in trouble for other misdemeanours such as taking the wrong course or mistaking the finishing line, too. Thankfully these cases are not too frequent, and usually end up with appeals and hearings in front of independent panels at the BHA headquarters in London.

The whip

Strict new rules concerning use of the whip were introduced in 2011, in order to improve racing's image to the outside world, and must be adhered to. While it is carried for safety and to correct a horse if it is not running straight (as in most other forms of equestrian activity), it is also used for encouragement in a finish. In a Flat race in Britain, a jockey can only strike a horse seven times, and eight times in a jumps race. In the heat of the moment, jockeys can go over that number. They will be ordered to explain why this is the case, and are usually given a brief suspension. The numbers of days jockeys are suspended for

▲ Jockeys must be careful not to overuse the whip, even in a close finish

misuse of the whip are recorded, and repeat offenders during a year will be hit with longer bans.

The whip can only be used by the jockey in a raised forehand position to the part of the horse that is behind them, not on its neck. It is not be to brought down from above the shoulder or applied with excessive force. The jockey must also be seen to give the horse time to respond from a strike of the whip, not use it quickly in succession. Mistreating a horse is, quite rightly, considered one of the gravest of offences.

Miscellaneous

Stewards can find themselves dealing with all manner of comings and goings on the track, from as serious as prohibited substances turning up in the stables, the wrong horse running in a race or a fight in the weighing room between jockeys, to as minor as a groom wearing the incorrect sponsorship branding.

NAPPER
BOOKMAKERS
On-Course

The betting

Racing and betting are inextricably linked. This undoubtedly contributes to the sport's somewhat louche reputation, but it need not conjure up images of shady dens of iniquity. A percentage of bookmakers' profits goes back into the sport via what has been known as a paying levy and as much as purists working within the industry would rather not associate themselves with something they might feel is a bit grubby, the simple fact is that racing would not exist without betting. Some £11 billion per year is wagered on British racing alone, after all.

Provided you gamble responsibly and only with what you can afford to lose, having a bet, or a 'punt' can enhance the enjoyment of a day's racing, or at least back up your judgement on choosing a horse. The cacophony of cheers during a race, as people follow their selection's rise or fall, and the hustle and bustle of the betting ring are what gives the racecourse its atmosphere.

Betting is also part of racing's enigmatic charm. There are the tales of great gambles landed, skulduggery and the punters who made their fortune and lost it again, all of which make their way into countless books and films.

Until 1961 and the legislation of off-course betting shops prompting a race to open them on high streets, the only way to bet on the races in Britain was to go to the track. If you were prepared to risk falling foul of the law you could use an illegal backstreet betting joint with its 'runners', sometimes children, who would relay bets back from the pubs.

Britain, Ireland and Australia are really the only countries that still have independent bookmakers on the racecourse, whereas elsewhere it is mostly state-run pool systems where bets are placed over the counter or on machines.

Latterly the Internet has taken over. The majority of betting turnover used to be on only horse racing and greyhounds, but this has fallen significantly since the promotion of football betting to the technology-savvy generation. Racing has had to work hard to make the product more attractive, with larger fields of runners, better odds and more accurate and well-explained statistics. A chief responsibility has been to ensure racing is well policed in order to address the popular misconception that it is all fixed.

The odds

The probability of a particular horse winning a race is reflected by its odds, which are usually displayed in the old-fashioned fractional form by bookmakers. Although they look confusing, a couple of rules of thumb make them easy to understand.

1.30 at Haynes Park

2–1	Sugar Lump
3–1	Clip Clop
4–1	Sad Ken
4–1	Horsing Around
20–1	Yourluckyday
100–1	Lost Cause

Should it pass the winning post in front, a £10 bet on Sugar Lump will win you: **2 x £10 + your original £10 = £30**

Clip Clop coming out ahead means: **3 x £10 + your original £10 = £40**

And should the unexpected happen and the longest odds horse Lost Cause (known as the 'outsider') do the business: **100 x £10 + your original £10 = £1,010**

More complicated odds

Odds can get a little more complicated, but the same rules apply:

2.00 at Haynes Park

1–2	Dead Cert
evens	Doubleyermoney
100–30	Mane Man
15–2	Why The Long Face

▲ A bookmaker advertises their odds on a digital board

Doubleyermoney will do exactly that, as 'evens' or 'even money' is the way of describing odds of 1–1. If he wins, a £10 bet will result in: **1 x £10 + your original £10 = £20**

Dead Cert, however, is the 'favourite' with the shortest odds in this race, and betting on him is not going to make you rich. In fact his odds are less than even money, so it is more likely he will win than he will lose. Verbally, rather than 1–2, his odds will be called 'two to one ON'.

A £10 winning bet on Dead Cert: **1–2 x £10 + your original £10 = £15**

And for Mane Man: **100–30 x £10 + your original £10 = £43.33**

Calculating the odds

The odds are not made up at random. Horses have different levels of ability and bookmakers are calculating the odds based upon the percentage chances of each one winning. In theory, the total percentage chance of all of the horses winning the race is 100%, and the individual fractions convert to percentages. Bookmakers are not that generous, so they build in a small margin called an 'overround' to give them a better chance of making a profit.

Having a bet

On-course bookmakers

Using an on-course bookmaker is the traditional way to have a flutter. The industry has had to adapt, firstly with the proliferation of betting shops around the country, and latterly from the advent of Internet betting, but it is still a colourful interaction dealing only in cold, hard cash. It can appear intimidating at first, but while bookmakers want to take your money off you, most pride themselves in gentlemanly behaviour and the personal touch, win or lose.

A bookmaker is like any other type of trader, managing their

▼ **Some bookmakers have their positions 'on the rails' between two enclosures**

profits and liabilities on bets, known as their 'book'. They will regularly shorten the odds of a horse when a considerable amount of money is taken on it, and lengthen the odds when they are proving unpopular. A bookmaker is constantly managing their odds and finances in order to guarantee a profit and make a living, reducing their liabilities by betting themselves with other bookmakers or off-course companies.

The odds offered by the bookmakers' stands will be largely the same, but the key is to keep your eyes open for the best offer and watch as they change. The odds at the time you place your bet are the odds you will receive if the horse wins, so if you see a bookmaker adjusting the odds on your selection downwards, jump in.

At major meetings, millions of pounds can be washing

around the betting area, or 'ring'. Some bookmakers are more interested in taking denominations of the paper variety but others will take smaller. This will be advertised on their stand. Take the slip in return, keep it safe, and bring it back if the bet is successful. The biggest firms, who take the largest bets, are usually along the border between the members' and grandstand enclosure, known as 'the rails'.

You can have two types of bet with a bookmaker. There is the standard win bet, as explained earlier. The other is the more complicated 'each-way' bet, which will also be on display as a sign and just needs to be asked for.

Each-way betting

This is when a bet is split into two parts. The first part is for the horse to win, and the second is for the horse to be placed (i.e. usually to finish in the first three depending upon how many runners there are).

Having an each-way bet provides more of a chance to get something back from the investment, as it is easier to pick a horse to finish in the first three than finding the winner. The place part is paid out at a fraction of the horse's odds, and varies according to the amount of runners in the race.

- **2–4 runners**
  A bet can only be to win
- **5–7 runners**
  1/4 the odds over 2 places (1st and 2nd place)
- **8–11 runners**
  1/5th the odds over 3 places (1st, 2nd and 3rd place)
- **12–15 runners**
  1/4 the odds over 3 places (1st, 2nd and 3rd place)
- **16 or more runners in handicap races only**
  1/4 the odds over 4 places (1st, 2nd, 3rd and 4th place)

It is generally more advantageous to bet each-way on bigger-priced horses, as they are less likely to win but might well finish placed.

Remember, if you ask for £10 each-way on Mr Ed at 16–1 in a race with many runners, it will cost £20 because of the two parts to the bet.

If Mr Ed wins, you collect: **£220**

16 x £10 + your original £10 = £170 (for the win part) (1/4 of 16) or 4 x £10 + your original £10 = £50 (for the place part)

If Mr Ed finishes second, third or fourth, the win part of the bet loses **£10**. However, you still collect **£50** from the place part of the bet.

Becoming a bookmaker

Some way apart from the caricature of the shady flat-capped geezers who run off with the cash as soon as the runners are off in the Derby, apart from honesty it actually takes a fair bit of paperwork and no mean investment to become a bookmaker.

Applicants will need to obtain a licence from the government's Gambling Commission, hold public liability insurance and obtain a certificate that they will be contributing to the levy. There is the purchase of the niche equipment, such as the stands and the boards that illustrate the odds, but what gets really expensive is where you want to be positioned. The prime places, known as pitches, are at the front of the stands,

▼ On-course bookmakers are still busy at big meetings, even if the industry has struggled after changing betting habits

where the largest footfall will be. The bigger the racecourse and potential market, the more they cost. Until the late 1990s, the pitches could not be bought or sold, and were simply passed on among bookmaking families. Only seniority allowed a rise up the pecking order.

Nowadays they can be traded via the Administration of Gambling on Tracks (AGT Ltd), which administers the betting ring. They will also deal with any lost or unclaimed betting tickets. Pitches are auctioned from time to time by the AGT. While a remote pitch at a small racecourse such as Wincanton in Somerset might only cost £100 to own, a place in the thick of the action at the Cheltenham Festival could be many, many thousands.

Bookmakers still enjoy the camaraderie of life around the tracks but it is hard work paying for assistants, daily entrance badges and various other expenses, especially on quiet midweek days. It is thought that there has been a rise in members who now only work on weekends or busy meetings.

Tic-tac

Before the days of electronic messaging and communication, bookmakers would pass on information to each other about the prices around the ring using a mysterious sign language and phrases developed from cockney rhyming and Victorian slang. They would often wear white gloves to be more visible. Tic-tac has largely become a lost art kept alive by the likes of bookmaker-turned-television personality John McCririck, a great historian of the betting ring.

Words such as 'neves' (seven backwards), 'carpet' (3–1) and Burlington Bertie (100–30) can still be heard in the ring if you listen hard enough, or look out for a few signs below if someone happens to be practising a bit of tic-tac.

TIC-TAC TALK

Evens (levels you devils) – Hands waggled up and down in opposite directions
6–4 (ear 'ole) – Back of right hand touches left ear
2–1 (bottle) – Right hand touches nose
9–4 (top of the head) – Both hands on the head
100–1 (century) – Pass both hands in front of the body

The betting shop

As on the high streets of Britain and Ireland, most racecourses also have a betting shop where you can do the same win and each-way bets, as well as more complicated varieties. Bets made here can also be collected in other shops belonging to the company. One main difference is that a bet is written on a slip and can be put on at the start of the day and left, whereas the bookmakers in the ring tend to deal on a race-by-race basis. You are given a copy to hold onto and return if there is anything to collect.

Secondly, there is a choice on the type of price you take. Many of the races will already have odds available on them, either on one of the screens, or by asking the manager behind the counter. If you prefer the look of the odds at that stage, you can ask to 'take the price', which will be recorded on the betting slip. Otherwise it will be left to what is known as the 'starting price' or 'SP', which is worked out by recording a sample of the odds from bookmakers at the racecourse at the time the race starts. These are the odds that are relayed back to the media and used to settle bets. Like everything, deciding whether to take the price or leave it to SP is very much a gamble.

Multiple bets

These can be done in betting shops and can be a low-investment way to win big, but this is far more difficult to achieve as they rely on the results of more than one race to go your way.

COMMON VARIETIES OF MULTIPLE BETS:

Trixie
3 selections (3 doubles on the different horses and one treble).
A £1 win trixie will cost £4.

Patent
3 selections (3 single bets, 3 doubles and one treble).
A £1 win patent will cost £7.

Yankee
4 selections (6 doubles, 4 trebles and an accumulator).
A £1 win yankee will cost £11.

Lucky 15
4 selections (4 single bets, 6 doubles, 4 trebles and an accumulator).
A £1 win lucky 15 will cost £15.

▶ Filling out a betting slip is incredibly simple

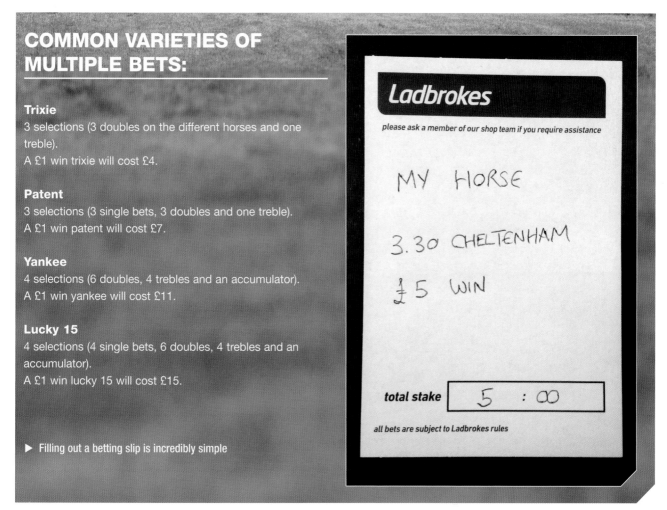

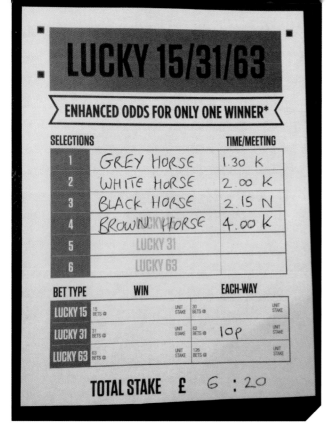

LUCKY 15/31/63

ENHANCED ODDS FOR ONLY ONE WINNER*

SELECTIONS		TIME/MEETING
1	GREY HORSE	1.30 K
2	WHITE HORSE	2.00 K
3	BLACK HORSE	2.15 N
4	BROWN HORSE	4.00 K
5	LUCKY 31	
6	LUCKY 63	

BET TYPE	WIN				EACH-WAY	
LUCKY 15	15 BETS @		UNIT STAKE	30 BETS @		UNIT STAKE
LUCKY 31	31 BETS @		UNIT STAKE	62 BETS @	10p	UNIT STAKE
LUCKY 63	63 BETS @		UNIT STAKE	126 BETS @		UNIT STAKE

TOTAL STAKE £ 6 : 20

▲ Adding selections into accumulators or multiples is a more adventurous method of betting

▼ A 'BETologist' offers help to American racegoers as to how to place their wagers (Keeneland Photo)

The simplest is a **double** on two horses in different races. The bet starts with the originally invested stake going onto one horse, and should it win, everything that was earned back rolls onto the second horse. This can be even more riskily tried as a **treble**, or with four horses or more, as an **accumulator**.

If you had a £1 accumulator on four horses that all won at odds of 2–1, you would get back £81. Of course, if just one horse loses, you get back nothing.

To ensure a better chance of a return, punters often do more complicated multiple bets. These can be done each-way as well, costing twice as much.

Ante-post betting

It is not only the day's racing on which odds are offered by bookmakers. Popular events, including the Cheltenham Gold Cup, Derby and a number of important handicaps, can be bet on throughout the year.

These 'ante-post' bets are a long shot, as there is no refund if the horse does not run in that particular race. The temptation, though, is that the odds are far bigger as they factor in possibilities such as the horse getting an injury, or regressing in the interim. Sometimes, if a horse does win a race, the trainer is reported as nominating a probable next target, and the punter can often have a bet on it there and

then. Before the days of 24-hour media and the compulsion for trainers to be more open with the public about their running plans for their horses, information was more on a need-to-know basis.

Barry Hills, who was once a stable lad for the British trainer John Oxley, was involved in the preparation of a horse called Frankincense for the 1968 Lincoln Handicap and had such confidence in him that he placed bet after bet on the horse from odds of 66–1 down to 100–8. Frankincense won, with Hills scooping around £60,000 (the modern equivalent of £1.5 million), which was enough for him to buy his own stable and become a highly accomplished trainer in his own right. The flow of information and paper trails means such a feat would be virtually impossible nowadays.

Pool (Tote) betting

Dotted around every racecourse, either inside the grandstand or in portable offices outside, are counters beneath screens with a variety of flashing numbers which look confusing, regardless of which country you are going racing in.

Some British tracks have now set up their own private ventures, but this way of betting has always been known as using the Tote, a name of the organisation which was run for more than 80 years by the government before being sold.

Tote betting can best be compared with the lottery. All of the money goes into a pool, the operating company takes its percentage, and the rest is divided amongst the winners. The system, known as pari-mutuel, was invented for betting in France back in 1870. The Tote offers simple win and each-way bets but you must wait until the result before knowing what the odds were – those displayed are the likely return but can easily change. Generally the odds of favourites are likely to be better with a bookmaker but, with fewer people actually placing money on them, outsiders can offer a far larger return on the Tote. As it is often the method used by the beginner, odds on horses with popular names are likely to be shorter on the Tote too.

Other pool bets

Exacta (forecast)

This involves picking the horses to finish first and second in the correct order, and because it is more difficult it can produce huge returns. Usually for a minimum stake of £2, it could be sensible to double up the bet to £4 and have what is known as a 'reverse' exacta, e.g. horse number 3 and horse number 6 to finish first and second in either order. You can add more horses in more complicated and expensive combinations.

PLACEPOT BETS

If you simply pick one horse per race, this bet will cost you £1. However, it is frustrating to choose a loser and go out in the very first leg, so most people add a few permutations, or 'lines'. Adding one more horse in one of the races doubles the amount of lines, and the more you add in multiples then the greater the sum you owe.

Fortunately this can be done in 10p increments, providing a total of £2 or more is staked.

So picking 2 horses in every race will be:
2 x 2 x 2 x 2 x 2 x 2 = 64 lines

At a 10p unit stake, the bet costs £6.40

The entire pool will then be shared amongst the number of successful tickets, depending on the size of each of their bets.

Trifecta

Much the same as the exacta, only involving picking the horses that finish first, second and third in the correct order for £2. Be careful not to accidentally pick too many combinations.

Placepot

On offer at every meeting, this is a low-investment way of trying to have an interest in each race and possibly land quite a big dividend. It involves ticking off the number of various horses on a coupon, which can look off-puttingly difficult at first, but isn't really.

The idea is to successfully get a placed horse in the first six races, following the same rules as each-way betting in that being placed means winning in races of four runners or less, or as much as finishing in the first four in handicaps with 16 runners or more (first three in non-handicap races).

The average dividend for a meeting according to recent Tote figures was around £400 to a £1 stake but the more people playing and the less predictable the results, the bigger it can be. It reached almost £92,000 at Cheltenham in December 2015.

Jackpot

The dreamer's bet, this requires picking the winner of six races on the day, which will either be at one selected meeting, or with races from several meetings. The minimum stake for a single line is £1, and more permutations can be added at 50p per line, provided a minimum of £2 is staked.

The jackpot pool starts at a minimum size of £10,000. If not won, it will roll over to the next day and can swell to a significant sum. It can sometimes become big enough to tempt

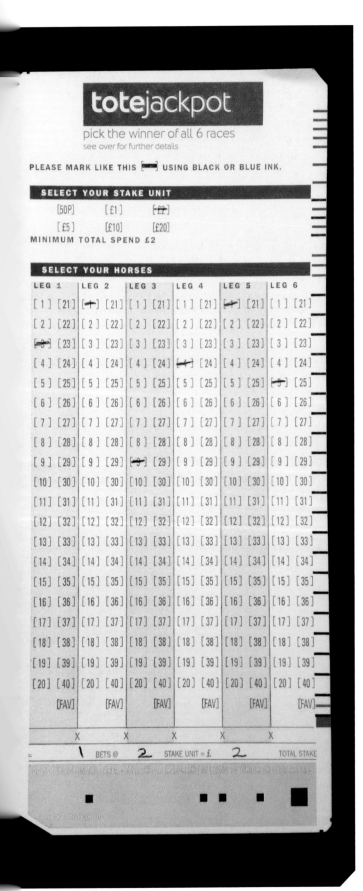

◄ A jackpot is a low-risk means of winning a potentially big payout, filling out one or more selections for each race on a slip

professional gamblers to lay out huge stakes and combinations in order to have a decent chance of scooping the lot, or even clubbing together with allies to form a syndicate. An average jackpot should pay about £16,000 to a £1 stake.

Scoop6

There have been additions over the years such as the Scoop6, a bet devised for televised races on a Saturday with a bonus that rolled on to the next weekend. It made a handful of small-staking millionaires, although the high-staking syndicates would hoover up most of the dividend when the pot rolled over a few times.

Pick 6

The equivalent to the jackpot is often known as 'Pick 6' around the world, and a favourite of American gamblers thanks to the occasional giant rollovers. Even in Dubai, where gambling is prohibited, there is usually a free Pick 6 where prizes are given out to winners. Overseas gamblers tend to be a little more adventurous in their methods of betting. Hong Kong, in particular, offers an almost overwhelming array of options involving picking numerous horses in certain orders.

Online betting

Any regular viewer of televised sport will be well aware of the proliferation of Internet betting companies offering odds on two raindrops sliding down a glass window, and consideration must be taken before opening an account and using it. Increasing pressure is being put on Internet bookmakers to make their behaviour more transparent.

With the innovations of mobile devices, it can still be a hassle-free way of having a bet at the races instead of having to fight through the crowds to the ring. Slick operators such as Paddy Power and Bet365 have made great strides in this genre with their slickly designed, easy-to-use sites and applications and will provide all of the types of wagers mentioned earlier and more.

The best thing for the customer is that all of these companies are baying for your attention and their prices can be different on an event, so it serves to shop around. A lot will also offer a free bet or some other sweetener to new account openers, and sometimes a reward to anyone that recommends them. It is obviously important to check what the terms and conditions are, as well as controlling the amount that you deposit, as money that is locked away online can sometimes feel fictional compared with hard cash. When starting out, it is safer to stick with one of the recognisable names, which also include William Hill, Ladbrokes, Coral or Victor Chandler, as there have been cases of fly-by-night operations that have disappeared and failed to honour bets.

As all of these bookmakers will offer slightly different odds on races, it has led to the evolution of comparison websites, such as www.oddschecker.com and www.bestbetting.com. Regularly updated, they pinpoint which are offering the biggest prices on each horse. Remember that for very little effort, you might find one company offering 8–1 whereas another is only offering 7–1, and for a £5 bet, that will be another £5 in the pocket if the horse wins.

Betting exchanges

In 1999, Andrew Black was to develop an idea that was to change the face of betting. Like the best ideas, it was incredibly simple yet effective. Black, something of a software genius and a keen gambler, had grown frustrated with the range of markets and odds that bookmakers offered, especially with regard to the Internet.

Black's concept was peer-to-peer betting; the idea that everyone could become a bookmaker. A customer could enter the odds and stake they wanted to have on a bet, and it could be accepted by someone else. Working with his business partner Ed Wray, they gathered investors from London and grew it from a tiny basement start-up to a commodity that floated for £1.4 billion on the Stock Exchange in 2010. Betfair offers opportunities to bet on hundreds of different sporting events, with racing from all over the world, and, once initiated, using it is easy.

Once the desired race has been accessed, the horses are listed vertically alongside their odds. In the left-hand column, in blue, are the decimal odds (including the stake) that the horse is available at to have a bet on, or to 'back', and on the right, in pink, are the odds it is available to take someone else's bet on, or to 'lay'.

Laying is, theoretically, easier as you only need that horse to be beaten, rather than win. However, that particular horse winning will incur a far heavier cost than backing it, as you have to multiply the stake by the odds. Luckily, the potential liability on the bet is flagged up before the transaction is confirmed, and must already have been deposited in the account.

Betfair, which has seen off plenty of potential rivals, takes a small percentage from each transaction. It has become very wealthy, due to the fact that it enticed millions of users. One of its major breakthroughs was offering a market even once a race was off. This so-called 'in-running' betting is for those with the sharpest minds and the quickest fingers, as the outcome of a race can change in a split second. There have been countless examples of horses coming from seemingly hopeless positions to win when a bet has been traded at Betfair's maximum odds of 999–1. Similarly, some have been beaten at the minimum 1.01, or 100–1 on.

▼ An exchange such as Betfair allows the opportunity to turn bookmaker and take as well as make bets *(Betfair)*

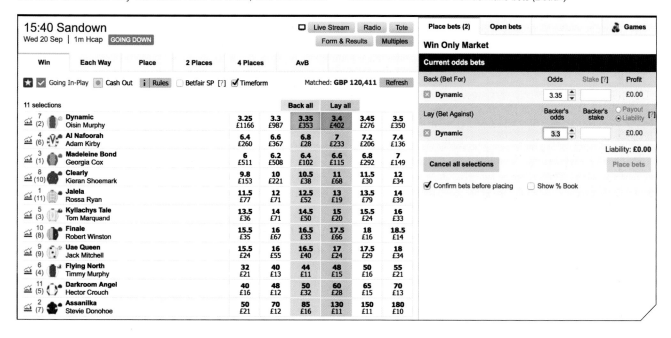

Picking a winner

▲ It is always a good idea to find a quiet corner of the racecourse for some form study

▼ Racing is lucky to be widely covered in the British media

The words 'beginners' luck' do ring true for some people, who spend a day at the races picking horses which have nice names or attractive grooms and end up leaving with far more money than they began with. Such a streak will not happen time and again, and in order to have a better chance of finding winners, there are a few variables to take into account. Solving races is a puzzle, studying the pros and cons of each runner and coming up with a list of the most likely contenders. There are occasional 100–1 winners that not even the horse's trainer sees coming, but more often than not there is a plausible reason for the result of a race.

Racecards from the track and newspapers will detail a horse's previous performances (with letters and numbers), while it is possible to dig deeper into it by going online and highlighting a particular race. There are always written comments on the horse's performance and sometimes a video replay. British and Irish racing has always been well served by the press, with almost all the national newspapers having a tipster providing selections in every race staged. Most at least list the runners and riders for the main meeting of the day and at the weekend, some tabloids have a pullout with a more detailed focus, which is a good source of sponsorship revenue from bookmakers. It is much the same in Australia, but in the rest of Europe and America coverage of racing in national papers is now almost non-existent, with information confined to specialist publications such as *Paris Turf* or the *Daily Racing Form* in America.

Specialist media

Racing Post

When going racing, it is helpful to have something more detailed and the *Racing Post* is the go-to resource. The national trade newspaper since 1986, it swallowed up its more venerable rival *The Sporting Life* and provides reams of statistics, in-depth form guides, tipsters and news on a daily basis. The *Post* is obviously dedicated reading for enthusiasts and professionals alike but should not be off-putting to the beginner and has keys and guides to explain its format. It has adapted to new technologies and mobile formats, with its website providing invaluable help for results, statistics, breeding and detailed records on individual horses, jockeys and trainers.

The Press Association

Britain's national news agency since 1868 has a form database that it uses to compile racecards, which are sent out to many newspapers and websites. It is in regular contact with racing bodies such as Weatherbys and the BHA to pass important notices on to the rest of the media and the public. Its information forms the body of betting and racing websites, which also provide their own content.

Timeform

A venerable institution formed in Halifax in 1948, this is the form guide favoured by the serious racing fan. Its main selling point is that a team of experts compiles its own ratings for each horse, which are adjusted according to the weight a horse has been allotted to carry and the type of race it is running in. The highest-rated on the Timeform figures is considered to be the most likely winner.

These can be studied alongside the Timeform comments and notes from a horse's previous runs in order to weigh up a considered selection. For the true die-hards, the company offers detailed time analysis of races and annuals with essays on high-profile horses, all written in its trademark dispassionate style. Timeform can be bought in various subscriptions for a few pounds a week and it now also sells its own premium racecards at racecourses, and these are not tailored to the connoisseur alone.

▲ **The go-to newspaper for stats and tipsters** *(Racing Post)*

Racing television

There have been various incarnations of racing channels since the mid-1990s and plenty of arguments about who owns the media rights to sell the product. All races in Britain and Ireland are now shown on several digital stations and live-streamed on the Internet, as well as in betting shops.

Through the last decade, these stations have been Racing UK and At The Races, which both contain a mixture of racing news, features, analysis and betting updates. The former is a subscription channel, with the latter falling loosely under the umbrella of Sky television.

Coverage of racing varies considerably from country to country. Major British and Irish racing events have been covered on terrestrial television since the coverage of live sport began, through the BBC, RTE and Channel 4 to an exclusive four-year deal with ITV, which commenced in 2017. The Grand National and the Derby, along with the likes of Wimbledon and the FA

▲ The studio at Racing UK, one of two dedicated daily racing television stations in Britain (*Racing UK*)

Cup Final, were included under a 1990 Broadcasting Act that protects certain key sporting events to be always shown on free-to-air television. Royal Ascot and the Cheltenham Festival are also considered events which will draw a large audience outside committed racing fans, and are covered extensively by dedicated general sports radio stations.

▼ Main racing events are covered by a variety of different media (*Racing UK*)

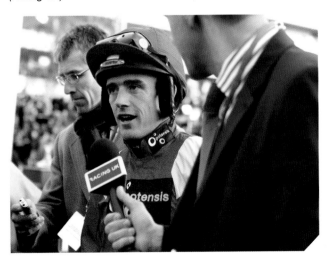

Studying the horses

A huge benefit of being at the races rather than watching it on television is that you get the chance to see the horses up close, and checking that they look well is just as important as their previous race record. Champions of the turf do often seem to be good-looking individuals, as they have fine genetics, but the point of this is not a beauty competition. Some might have a pronounced scar or an ugly white mark on its head, but those

▼ It is a race not a beauty contest, but presentation is important. There is often a cash prize for the groom with the 'best turned out' horse

are not hindrances to them running well. When standing in the paddock watching the horses before a race, it is important to assess the animal's condition and behaviour, looking for signs. As with buying a horse, finding one that is big, strong and in proportion should mean that you can feel confident that it will give a good run for the money.

In the paddock

Good signs

Look for a horse that appears to be a healthy athlete – it will stand out in comparison with the unhealthy ones. It should have bright eyes and shining skin, particularly around the neck and hindquarters, and the sun will glint off it on a clear day. Similarly, dull-looking skin can mean the horse is not at its best. Immaculate hooves, plaited manes and tails or even patterns brushed onto their coats are pure aesthetics, but at least proof that the horse is being well looked after.

Fitness can be measured too – with a fit horse you always have a chance of winning. On a fit horse, you will be able to see a few ribs showing through around its middle and real muscle

▼ The paddock offers an opportunity to look at the horses that you do not get on the television

definition, particularly with a line that runs down its hindquarters. The horse needs to be alert and walking purposefully around the paddock, but not looking around too much – this is a sign that it is still inexperienced.

Bad signs

An anxious horse is not one that is going to perform at its best, as it is using up its energy before it has even started racing. A telltale sign is when it starts sweating, particularly when a white lather shows up its back legs. Some horses do sweat habitually, especially on a warm day, and run fine, so discarding them can occasionally be a lesson learned, but it is generally taken as a negative.

Allow them a little bit of jig-jogging from foot to foot, but a horse doing this constantly as it walks around the ring is not a positive. Doing this to excess, tossing their heads or playing up with their handler, also means they are exerting themselves too much, too soon.

An unfit horse will have a clearly softer look to it than a fit horse. A particularly unfit one will have a bit of a tummy on it (not to be confused with the size of its ribcage), and clearly needs a few races to get into better shape. Bandages, particularly on the front legs, are not considered a positive as they can hint at a physical issue.

◄ It is important that a horse heads to the start in an orderly manner like this, instead of misbehaving

most likely run its race already. Breaking into a gallop that the jockey cannot control will have the same effect.

Seeing the horse going to the start gives us our first idea of how the horse runs, too. Watch how they use their front legs. A horse that seems to just skim lightly over the ground, known in the trade as a 'daisy cutting' action, will usually be better running over a faster surface. One with more of a 'knee action', where it lifts the knee high and hits the ground hard, looking more as if it runs in an up-and-down type of way, should be better able to plough through softer ground than others. There is a school of thought that horses with bigger feet go better on softer ground, but this is not the conclusion of an extensive scientific survey.

Typically enough, some horses can look completely wonky and still have ability. There can only ever be pointers to picking a winner, not hard and fast rules.

Studying the form

Studying the form includes taking into account all manner of factors that can contribute to a horse winning a race, and it is a necessary pleasure of going to the races. Everyone has their own method, from simple hunches to complicated statistical systems. Form itself essentially means the horse's past record and can be broken down into further sections. Being 'in form' is a phrase that has slipped into general parlance and describes a horse that has been winning recently, while one that has not been performing like its usual self becomes 'out of form'.

Heading to the start

Horses need to warm up before running with a canter down to the start. By observing this and the horse's interaction with its jockey, you can get more signs of its chances. Again, they can behave differently, but it is important to see them progressing into a controlled canter, moving steadily and not fighting the rider.

This is a time when the race can easily be lost. Throwing off a jockey and running loose will mean, provided that it can be caught and passes an inspection allowing it to start, that it has

FOLLOWING YOUR HORSE

You should be able to see your horse in the race, either on the big television screen or with your own eyes, but sometimes you need to rely on the commentary over the speaker system. Commentators have to make it past an expert panel before they can join the national rota and, by and large, keep their explanation clear and concise. Sometimes, though, they slip into racing vernacular, such as the following:

Bowling along – horse is moving nicely (usually in the lead).
Wagging the tail – horse is in last place.
Out with the washing – horse is now a long way behind.
Scraping the paint – horse is keeping close to the rail.
Stuck behind a wall of horses – horse's route to the front is blocked.

◀ Studying the form is an important part of a day at the races (*Racing Post*)

they ought to be able to perform somewhere near their expected level – it is an old racing cliché that a top-class horse will handle any ground. However, a deluge of rain will suddenly enhance the chances of a soft ground specialist that has previously shown a higher level of performance in muddier conditions.

There is more difficulty with younger horses when they are untried on particular ground, but the trainer has decided to take the chance in running them. It is usually a case of trial and error, and a horse can be forgiven a disappointing run if the ground was very different to what they were used to. Ground officially rated around good should be safe for all horses, but it is when it gets much drier or wetter that particular animals come into their own. Modern all-weather surfaces are considered suitable for all horses to perform well on.

The ground

The state of the ground is the first piece of the puzzle to note. It can change rapidly in times of extreme weather, and cause plenty of horses to become non-runners when trainers decide they are unwilling to risk them in different conditions, so it is important to know the up-to-date going. With experienced horses, it should be taken on trust that if they are taking part,

Recent form

A horse that has been running well in recent weeks with a selection of wins or respectable placings to its name is as good an indication as there is to it running well again, as it has proved that it is fit, healthy and enjoying its job.

It should be taken as a less encouraging sign if a horse has not run for 100 days or more. It might have had a health problem or an injury, or simply have been given a holiday. Either way, there is a fair chance that the horse will not be performing at its maximum capability on this occasion. This does not matter if the horse is far better than its opponents and should win anyway, but it could be a chink in the armour of a short-priced favourite.

Some horses do run best with their races widely spaced out, usually described as 'going well fresh', and the evidence for this will be in the form. Some trainers also pride themselves in being able to prepare a horse to win 'fresh' at the first attempt, which is more down to knowledge one will pick up with experience.

Particular warning signs in jumps races are for a horse that has fallen or unseated its rider regularly (it will probably be a bad jumper) or fallen recently (it might have lost its confidence).

▼ Trainer Paul Nicholls and his team check the ground to ensure it is suitable for their runners

Ascot Racecourse is giving a prize of £300 to the lad or girl responsible for the best turned out horse, and a prize of £300 to the lad or girl responsible for the winning horse.

The Hardwicke Stakes
(Group 2)

itv RACING

One Mile About Four Furlongs (2,300 metres)
For Four Yrs Old And Upwards

Stalls - Inside

(Class 1) **Total prize fund £225000**
(FOR CONDITIONS OF THIS RACE SEE PAGE 70)

totetrifecta

Owners Prize Money. Winner £100260; Second £41153; Third £20588; Fourth £10283; Fifth £5153; Sixth £2565. (Penalty Value £127597.50) A SS

	Form	Owner	Trainer Age	st lb	(lbs)

1 ACROSS THE STARS (IRE) (35)   4 9 1   (127)
13013-5   B c Sea The Stars (IRE) - Victoria Cross (IRE) (Mark of Esteem (IRE))
MR SAEED SUHAIL   Olivier Peslier
SIR MICHAEL STOUTE, Newmarket
(Breeder - Hascombe and Valiant Studs)
DRAW **9**
CD   ROYAL BLUE, YELLOW chevron, YELLOW cap, ROYAL BLUE spots.
Won the King Edward last season and ended his 3-y-o campaign with a fine third in Great Voltigeur. Should be straighter for his Newbury return but needs to take a big step forward to figure here.
Star Rating★★★☆☆Official BHA Rating 113

2 ARTHENUS (57)   5 9 1   (127)
40210-6   B g Dutch Art - Lady Hen (Éfisio)
A. COOMBS & J. W. ROWLEY   Tom Queally
JAMES FANSHAWE, Newmarket
(Breeder - Brook Stud Bloodstock Ltd)
DRAW **5**
C   EMERALD GREEN, PURPLE seams, MAUVE sleeves, EMERALD GREEN and PURPLE hooped cap.
Developed into a smart performer last season, winning a Listed event at Saint-Cloud, but was well-held on return at Sandown in April and looks up against it in this company.
Star Rating★☆☆☆☆Official BHA Rating 108

3 BARSANTI (IRE) (28)   5 9 1   (127)
13212-3   B g Champs Elysees - Silver Star (Zafonic (USA))
SHEIKH MOHAMMED OBAID AL MAKTOUM   Andrea Atzeni
ROGER VARIAN, Newmarket
(Breeder - Glenvale Stud)
DRAW **14**
D BF   YELLOW, large BLACK spots and spots on cap.
Progressed well in 2016, scoring 4 times in handicap company. Solid third in Listed contest on return but in much deeper water here and makes limited appeal.
Star Rating★★☆☆☆Official BHA Rating 108

The Hardwicke Stakes (Group 2) - continued

	Form	Owner	Trainer Age	st lb	(lbs)

4 CHEMICAL CHARGE (IRE) (35)   5 9 1   (127)
222-126   Ch h Sea The Stars (IRE) - Jakonda (USA) (Kingmambo (USA))
QATAR RACING LIMITED   Oisin Murphy
RALPH BECKETT, Kimpton Down
(Breeder - Viktor Timoshenko)
DRAW **12**
D   CLARET, GOLD braid, CLARET sleeves, CLARET cap, GOLD tassel.
Made successful return at Doncaster in April and fine effort in defeat in John Porter at Newbury subsequently. Ran below-par over same C&D last time, however, and it's easy enough to look elsewhere. STEWARDS NOTE: Following its run on 20/5/2017 it was reported that the horse did not face the visor.   Star Rating★☆☆☆☆Official BHA Rating 111

5 DAL HARRAILD (28)   4 9 1   (127)
3131-61   Ch g Champs Elysees - Dalvina (Grand Lodge (USA))
ST ALBANS BLOODSTOCK LIMITED   Pat Cosgrave
WILLIAM HAGGAS, Newmarket
(Breeder - St Albans Bloodstock LLP)
DRAW **6**
D   BRONZE.
Improved last season, rounding campaign off with Newmarket Listed win over this trip in September. Upped his game further when taking York Listed race last time and is one of the likelier contenders.
Star Rating★★★☆☆Official BHA Rating 111

6 DARTMOUTH (36)   5 9 1   (127)
11322-1   B h Dubawi (IRE) - Galatee (FR) (Galileo (IRE))
THE QUEEN   Ryan Moore
SIR MICHAEL STOUTE, Newmarket
(Breeder - Darley)
DRAW **4**
CD   PURPLE, GOLD braid, SCARLET sleeves, BLACK velvet cap, GOLD fringe.
Very smart performer who completed a hat-trick in pattern company when taking this race last year. Shaped as if retaining all his ability when landing Yorkshire Cup on return and holds obvious claims.
Star Rating★★★★☆Official BHA Rating 118

7 IDAHO (IRE) (22)   4 9 1   (127)
321U5-6   B c Galileo (IRE) - Hveger (AUS) (Danehill (USA))
MR M. TABOR, D. SMITH & MRS JOHN MAGNIER   Seamie Heffernan
AIDAN O'BRIEN, Ireland
(Breeder - Hveger Syndicate)
DRAW **7**
D   ROYAL BLUE, ORANGE disc, striped sleeves and cap.
Brother to Highland Reel who gained reward for his consistency when landing Great Voltigeur at York last August. Shaped encouragingly on return in Coronation Cup and has to enter calculations.
Star Rating★★★★☆Official BHA Rating 117

8 MUNTAHAA (IRE) (36)   4 9 1   (127)
314-310   Gr c Dansili - Qertaas (IRE) (Linamix (FR))
MR HAMDAN AL MAKTOUM   Jim Crowley
JOHN GOSDEN, Newmarket
(Breeder - Shadwell Estate Company Limited)
DRAW **1**
D   ROYAL BLUE, WHITE epaulets, striped cap.
Dual winner last term and resumed progress this season with determined success in John Porter at Newbury in April. Ran as if amiss at York last time, though, and needs to bounce back. STEWARDS NOTE: Following its run on 19/5/2017 it was reported that the horse would prefer a quicker surface.   Star Rating★★☆☆☆Official BHA Rating 113

How To Read Your Racecard

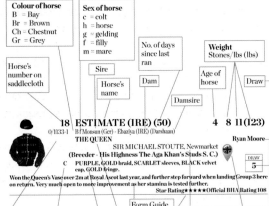

Colour of horse	**Sex of horse**
B = Bay	c = colt
Br = Brown	h = horse
Ch = Chestnut	g = gelding
Gr = Grey	f = filly
	m = mare

No. of days since last ran

Weight Stones/lbs (lbs)

Horse's number on saddlecloth

Sire

Age of horse

Draw

Horse's name

Dam

Damsire

18 ESTIMATE (IRE) (50)   4 8 11 (123)
0/1133-1   B f Monsun (Ger) - Ebaziya (IRE) (Darshaan)
THE QUEEN   Ryan Moore
SIR MICHAEL STOUTE, Newmarket
(Breeder - His Highness The Aga Khan's Studs S. C.)
DRAW **5**
C   PURPLE, GOLD braid, SCARLET sleeves, BLACK velvet cap, GOLD fringe.
Won the Queen's Vase over 2m at Royal Ascot last year, and further step forward when landing Group 3 here on return. Very much open to more improvement as her stamina is tested further.
Star Rating★★★★☆Official BHA Rating 108

Form Guide

Owner

Trainer and location of training establishment

Country where horse is trained

Owner's Colours

C = Course winner	
CD = Course & Distance Winner	
D = Distance winner	
BF = Beaten favourite	

Star Rating Explained
Each horse has been given a star rating, these are defined below:
★★★★★ Selected to win the race.
★★★★☆ Good chance of being placed.
★★★☆☆ By no means out of the reckoning but at least one or two hold stronger claims.
★★☆☆☆ Unlikely to win but not totally without hope.
★☆☆☆☆ Can be given little or no chance.

Jockey's Name
If there is a number next to the name, this indicates that the jockey can claim that amount in weight (lbs) off the stated riding weight

Previous Performances
/ = denotes new season
– = denotes new year
d = disqualified
r = ran out
U = unseated rider
P = pulled up

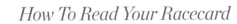

▲◄◄ **A horse's latest form is helpfully outlined in the racecard available from the track**

Being 'pulled-up', when the jockey has taken the horse out of the race before the finish, is not encouraging either.

Beware too of horses with sequences of seconds in their form. This 'seconditis', as it is known colloquially, suggests a horse has ability but is reluctant to go the extra yard and actually win. These 'ungenuine' horses will find a way of losing a race at whatever level they run in and are not to be trusted.

Course form

Whether a horse has performed well at this particular racecourse in the past is a very important factor to take into account. It is less applicable in countries with more uniform-shaped courses, such as America, but there is great variety to the tracks in Britain and Ireland. Venues such as the undulating Brighton and tight Chester are suited to certain horses that return there time and again to win. Sometimes this is because their physical build lends itself to it, or because the ground is usually similarly fast or slow there, but often it can be far harder to define quite why.

So-called 'course specialists' can be extreme; a horse called

▲ Previous course form is a helpful asset

Rapporteur won an impressive 19 races at Lingfield in the early 90s, yet never got his head in front anywhere else. He was later rewarded with an event named in his honour at the Surrey track. Meanwhile Risk Of Thunder, owned by James Bond actor Sean Connery, won the La Touche Cup cross-country race at Punchestown a staggering seven times. The apparently obscure names of some racecourse bars around the country are often in memory of other equine heroes.

Horses cannot explain why they like certain places, but neither are they known for their rational thinking. It could be because of the smell of the air, or simply feeling reassured that they are somewhere in which they have had a good experience before.

Jump horses can exhibit marked tendencies on tracks that run either clockwise or anti-clockwise, going markedly left or right over the fences and losing valuable ground. From this point, they will stick to tracks that go one particular way. If a horse is running at a course that shares characteristics with a course it has done well at in the past, for instance with an uphill finish or sharp turns, then there is a valid reason to think it can replicate its effort that day.

Distance form

It can take a while for a trainer to find out the ideal distance for their horse. They will usually start off over shorter races when they are younger and find their feet; often it is a case of trial and error.

If a horse has registered a previous win, or at least performed well over the race distance, this is certainly a plus when considering a selection. Should a horse be stepping up or down in distance from its previous race, whether this will help it to win is an educated guess.

Look at the sort of change it entails. A jumper (the equine equivalent of a marathon runner) that races over three miles clearly has stamina, and a quarter of a mile either way should not make a whole lot of difference.

For a speedier Flat horse, there can be finer margins. Step it up the same distance from a mile to ten furlongs and the petrol gauge could run down very quickly, but drop it down six furlongs and it could look far too slow. Compare it with a human 200-metre specialist runner trying to be as effective over 400 and 100 metres.

Clues are in how the horse has been running previously. If it appears to have got tired towards the end of a race, a drop in distance could suit it. If it seems to have been outpaced in the

▲ **Not every horse will last the distance** *(Keeneland Photo)*

middle of a race before finding a second wind, it might be better off running over slightly further. Of course, the horse might just be plain slow at any distance!

When there is less evidence of previous runs by horses just starting out, or those who have only raced a few times, the pedigree comes more into the equation. If a close relative performed well over a particular distance it is likely, if not certain, that this horse will be suited to it too.

The rating

Every horse is assigned a rating by a team of handicappers, with the numbers equating to imperial pounds. The handicappers watch every horse's individual performance, looking at the general standard of the race, the positions in which the horses finished and how the race was run. In Britain and Ireland, they weigh a number of variables up and publish a figure, also known as an official handicap mark. Unless they win on their first or second career start, all horses must run three times in maiden or novice races before they can be assigned a mark so that the handicapper has a reasonable idea of its ability.

These ratings will then go up when a horse has been running well and it will carry more weight next time. The ratings will drop when a horse is considered by the handicappers to be running below the level they believe it is capable of. In a race where the horses all carry level weights, the one with the highest rating is considered by these experts to be the best and should theoretically win.

Sometimes it is that easy, but interest in betting would have waned pretty dramatically if this were always the case. Ratings

BANDING IN HANDICAPS

Horses with similar ratings are banded together in handicaps in order to make them more competitive:

Flat horses are rated between 0 and 140
Jump horses are rated between 0 and 175

So assume the brilliant jumper Sprinter Sacre, who was rated 188 at his peak in 2013, was entered in a handicap against a moderate horse rated 78 called Mr Slowcoach.

Mr Slowcoach would carry the minimum allowed weight of 10st
Sprinter Sacre would carry 110lbs (7st 12lb) more – or 17st 12lb.

As the maximum weight horses are allowed to carry is usually 11st 12lb, this would be a total mismatch and Sprinter Sacre would win easily.

▼ Sprinter Sacre had one of the highest ratings in the history of jump racing

become very significant when it comes to handicap races. The highest-rated horse in the race carries the most weight, and the others carry a pound less for the amount they are rated inferior.

The class

A horse could have several wins next to its name in its recent form, but that might not tell the whole story. If the win was achieved in a humble selling race, even if the horse enjoyed a comfortable victory, this is not a guarantee that it will be able to fare as well in a handicap or an open race. Winning a Class 5 level handicap might then entitle it to jump into a Class 4 the next time, but the question in the mind must be whether it has improved enough to win a better race.

These decisions must be taken when looking at when horses from maidens go into handicaps, or from handicaps go up into Group or Graded races. Beware of horses that have been performing moderately in better races and have dropped down. Sometimes they will take advantage of an easy opportunity, other times the horse only appears to have an easier opportunity and is unlikely to recover from a downward spiral in fortune. The best trainers are clever at placing their horses in the right races.

At the fashionable occasions such as Royal Ascot, horses are sometimes run in races they have no realistic chance of winning simply because the owner wants a social day out.

Solving a handicap

We are dealing with half a ton of horse, so the difference of a few pounds of lead on its back should not appear to make much difference. According to the way the BHA handicappers work out their figures, it has less of an effect over shorter distances, and can be measured by the following scale:

On the Flat

5f	3lbs per length
6f	2.5lbs per length
7–8f	2lbs per length
9–10f	1.75lbs per length
11–13f	1.5lbs per length
14f	1.25lbs per length
15f+	1lb per length

It is assumed that in long-distance jump races, 1lb of weight equals one horse length during the course of a race. In essence, this means that the best/top-rated horse has a better chance of conceding weight to its rival in shorter races. One should always consider the merits of the top weight in a handicap first before looking at the others in the race.

The key for most punters for solving a handicap, though, is to find a reason why a horse could be able to win from the mark it has on a given day. An improving horse might have won from a low mark but still have enough potential to overcome the extra weight from a revised mark. Some have simply reached the right level and should run well without necessarily winning. Horses that are just starting out in handicaps can turn out to be either under- or over-estimated in terms of the mark they are given, as the handicapper has fairly little knowledge of them.

Another horse might have been struggling in races before some leniency from the handicapper and been dropped down to a mark at which it has won from before. This will often be referred to as being 'on a good mark'.

The mark of a horse is part of an ongoing game between handicapper and trainer. Running a horse when it is not fully fit, or at unsuitable distances and tracks or using inexperienced jockeys so it does not perform as well are some of the legal tactics a trainer can use in order for a horse to receive a more favourable mark. The handicapper is obviously aware of all these tricks.

▼ The more weight in the saddlecloth, the harder the task for horse and jockey

Trainer form

This is a vital point to consider. The importance of a jockey tends to be exaggerated in the media, even if they can occasionally perform miracles by simply staying on, or producing their mount to win with split-second precision.

One talented ex-jockey once explained in private that 90% of winning a race was about the ability of the horse, a view which is broadly shared by other experts. The vast majority of riders, certainly in the major nations, are competent at the main requirements of getting their horse to start properly, settle it down in the race, follow tactics and find and take their opportunity. But if it is their conveyance that has the off day, there is nothing that they can do.

It is worth checking how a trainer's recent runners have been doing, either by using a search engine or highlighting their name on an online racecard. Provided some of them have performed adequately over the previous 14 days or so, this is not enough to deter from choosing a horse, but if a large number have been finishing a long way behind, or if they have had very few runners comparative to the size of their stable, it could be a concern. It does not really matter if 100–1 chances are defeated, as that would be expected, but alarm bells should ring if they have had a number of short-priced runners or favourites getting beaten.

Some sort of illness might have affected their horses, or the horses' fitness could have been set back by bad weather, so it might be advisable to look for another selection. Conversely, some trainers can hit spectacular runs of form, similar to a striker who cannot stop scoring goals. Good health can be as contagious as poor health in a stable and horses on long losing runs with no apparent chance of success can start winning. The leading trainers will aim to maintain their form for most of the year, but they all have peaks and troughs.

▲ The jockey is important – but the horse even more so

▼ The draw can be crucial in the outcome of a Flat race

Thursday 7th July 2016; 15:15
One Mile and about Four Furlongs
The Princess Of Wales' Arqana Racing Club Stakes (Group 2) (Class 1) (3yo+)

Official Finish Time: 02:29.93

Sectional Times

	Draw	11f	10f	9f	8f	7f	6f	5f	4f	3f	2f	1f	WP
3 Big Orange	5	14.88	13.51	11.61	12.51	13.47	12.84	12.89	11.66	11.55	11.33	11.26	12.42
6 The Grey Gatsby	4	15.61	13.90	11.98	12.44	13.42	12.77	13.01	11.70	10.89	11.09	11.10	12.43
1 Exosphere	6	15.08	13.90	11.59	12.54	13.44	12.76	13.08	11.57	11.35	11.25	11.24	12.63
2 Battersea	1	15.50	14.20	12.03	12.47	13.43	12.82	12.98	11.68	10.88	11.02	11.36	12.63
5 Second Step	7	15.04	13.72	11.59	12.50	13.44	12.75	13.09	11.53	11.51	11.44	11.48	13.02
4 Elite Army	3	15.31	13.89	11.65	12.51	13.41	12.79	13.06	11.52	11.46	11.13	11.45	13.05
7 Muntazah	2	15.34	14.07	11.77	12.51	13.43	12.74	13.02	11.63	11.22	11.13	11.75	13.55

This data has been provided by TurfTrax Ltd courtesy of Newmarket Racecourses Ltd.
Terms & conditions apply to the use of this data please contact TurfTrax Ltd or Racecourse Media Group/Racing UK for more details.

The draw

Whilst the use of stalls for Flat races is to ensure that runners start in a straight line, this does not mean they necessarily have an even chance.

Stalls are numbered and positions are allocated at random in Britain by racing's secretariat, Weatherbys, or for very occasional big races there are lottery-style events in which contestants can pick their number. The number is known as your 'draw'. The lowest number is the stall closest to the inside rail of a racecourse, whether they go clockwise or anticlockwise around it. As it is not a staggered start similar to a 400m athletics race, it can be a clear advantage to have a low draw on a track with bends, as the horse on the inside in stall one is travelling a shorter distance than the horse in stall 16.

This is most marked in sprint races around tight bends and becomes less important over longer distances, especially when there are few runners, as jockeys have time to find a position. In a larger field, it can be more difficult for a jockey to move across and get into the pack, and there are regular hard-luck stories with horses wasting energy when stuck on the outside.

Sprint races on a straight track can be even more confusing. The ground can vary even within a width of 30m, and differ from day to day, for factors such as soil make-up or where watering machines are placed, and big fields will frequently split as soon as the stalls open, with two or three different groups across the track.

Jockeys and trainers will walk and assess the course before the meeting to see where they think the fastest ground is. If high numbered stalls dominate the finish to one race, it is an idea to concentrate on those in another race at a similar distance. Serious form students will also consider the tactics. A proliferation of likely front runners on one side of the draw means that is where the action will probably happen even at the finish.

The time

All races are timed and published. They can then be compared with a standard time over that particular course and distance to decide whether a race was particularly fast or slow. Some organisations, as well as individuals, process their own 'speed

▲ Sectional timing gives a highly accurate breakdown of the pace of the race (Turftrax/RMG)

figures', which compare performances with the standard time and come up with a rating to use next time. By and large, it is a pursuit best suited to those with an analytical mind and a head for figures. Still, it is always worth remembering that only a good horse can run a fast time; both bad and good horses can run slow times.

In Asia and North America, the use of the even more complicated sectional timing is in wider use. This involves every horse carrying a timing chip and breaking the times of each runner down to furlong or even 100m sections. The numbers are then crunched to see what the pace of the race was like at different stages and how a horse has expended its energy throughout a race. They are regarded as an invaluable piece of factual evidence by some, but are complicated to grasp to begin with.

Beyond the obvious

It is sensible to start with the clear checklist of earlier factors, but there are many other hints as to why a horse might win a race and many successful punters rely on becoming familiar with individual horses and the modus operandi of trainers and jockeys. Unless they tell you themselves that they are expecting them to run well, much of this is far more about hunches and reading between the lines. There is no such thing as a guaranteed winner in racing, even if it is a very short-priced favourite, and it can pay to think outside the box.

Look at whether a horse has travelled a long distance from its stable to the racecourse. It is expensive for the owner to be paying for the mileage and might suggest that the trainer has picked the race because it gives the horse its optimum chance of winning something. It augurs well if that owner and trainer have made the journey themselves, as they could be expecting to be collecting a prize. In contrast, of course, a trainer also likes to have winners at their local course, as it is more likely their owners will be able to attend and go home happy.

Note if a top jockey has come to a track for just one or

two rides – it is likely that this is because the trainer has told them that their horse will run well. The leading names do not want to spend hours in the car for nothing. Sometimes the top jockey has been booked for one horse over another he could perhaps also have ridden in the same race, and that can be a clue in itself.

Consider the horse itself. Is it wearing blinkers for the first time and could they have a positive effect? Has it run best when its races have been spaced out, or does it have a particularly good record when ridden by a particular jockey? It could even be something as spurious as an owner sponsoring a race in which they have a runner. They are going to be even keener to win it, and are likely to have their horse primed to show their best. Many of these reasons can look blindingly obvious after the event, but it is always more satisfying to have spotted something others have missed.

Using tipsters

Just as it is easy to be bombarded with correspondence from those who claim to have the secrets to trading shares or pyramid schemes, there are those who will boast that they have cracked the racing game and are providing winner after winner through telephone lines, social media or subscription services. The natural instinct is to beware of all, if not necessarily for fear of false advertising, but for the small print of charges, difficulty of severing any contract, or even having to put a bet on for the provider as payment.

▲ Sometimes, even after intensive study to pick the right horse, it just isn't your day

One of the pleasures of racing is using one's own judgement and gaining knowledge, and in any event, there are no end of informed articles in the media where someone provides their view. The *Racing Post* and some other outlets publish a 'naps table', where the main newspaper tipsters provide their best selection of the day. Profits or losses are recorded, and this is a simple and free way to at least find a pointer from someone who knows what they are doing.

▼ It is more fun to trust your own judgement than follow tipsters

Professional gamblers

In the days before regularly televised racing, there would be a community who would go from track to track, earning their living from betting. There is a huge advantage in actually seeing the horses running, building up a mental archive and learning from the racing grapevine, rather than simply looking at the form.

Some were characters that are still celebrated today, such as Alex Bird, who would stand by the winning line and trust his judgement on which horse won – a photo finish would take a few minutes to develop after the war and Bird made a fortune by being a step ahead and getting his bets on while the bookmakers were still trading on the result.

Those days are now largely gone, replaced by home-based traders who have to function more like accountants. Perhaps more scarily there are also technology whizzes who design systems to detect minuscule variations in the markets and automatically place bets. Although only tiny percentages are regular and sizeable winners, they do exist. Many will have started betting in £1 and £2 amounts and showed an aptitude for it, and there are tales that the biggest fish turn over millions in a year.

The most successful keep their methods and profit secret. The majority of those that have agreed to be interviewed in the press tend to specialise in certain kinds of races, perhaps two-year-olds or novice hurdles, and learn about the horses intimately; there are simply too many races to have even passing knowledge of all of them. Professional gambling requires starting off with a big deposit and a controlled plan on stakes, in order to withstand losing runs. They trust themselves enough to know when the odds of a horse are bigger than they should be, and back their judgement accordingly. As bookmakers are not keen on regular winners and reserve the right to close an account, one of the biggest challenges for a gambler is to keep finding ways of getting their money on at the right odds.

The legend of Barney Curley

A Northern Irishman who managed bands in his time and once trained as a Jesuit priest is perhaps the most venerated name in the lores of gambling. The fedora-wearing Barney Curley is infamous for laying out a betting coup in 1975 on a horse named Yellow Sam, which he owned. He knew Yellow Sam would win a small jumps race and picked an obscure Irish track called Bellewstown, which had only one telephone.

▲ **Barney Curley** *(Getty Images)*

Curley had recruited a team of people to wait in numerous betting shops and a few minutes before the race, his network delivered the instructions. Crucially, an accomplice monopolised the phone talking to a fictional dying aunt so the bookmakers could not get any word over to the track of the developing gamble in order to reduce their liabilities and the official starting price. Yellow Sam won at 20–1 despite being a virtual certainty and netted Curley £300,000, still a huge sum now but staggering in the 1970s.

He was to become a racehorse trainer and almost 40 years later, orchestrated another coup as audacious and complex in its conception as the previous. One quiet January day in 2010, in an operation months in the planning, Curley prepared three of his own horses and one now in another trainer's care, to run. They were combined in numerous multiple bets in small enough denominations so as not to alert the bookmakers, which have mechanisms in place when large numbers of bets on certain horses are being placed close together. Three of them won, claiming the sting £4 million, which would have risen to at least £15 million if Sommersturm had not disappointed.

Curley claims it was only ever for the challenge and to give bookmakers a taste of their own medicine. He has dedicated himself to years of charity work in Zambia and is a mentor to such riding luminaries as Frankie Dettori and Jamie Spencer.

The racecourses

There are 60 racecourses to choose from in Great Britain, including some of the best known in the world, with another 26 in Ireland, and visiting just these would be enough to keep anyone occupied. One of the joys of following racing as a hobby, though, is its internationality and the sport has been replicated across six continents with broadly the same rules. The International Federation of Horseracing Authorities (IFHA) has 59 member countries, where details can be mostly be found for how to attend a race meeting anywhere from Chad to Barbados or Peru.

Racing in Britain

Many more racecourses existed in the 18th, 19th and 20th centuries than those found in Britain today. Plenty were part of towns and cities, but have now been swallowed up by development. There was even one at Gatwick until 1940 on what is now the airport, with only a couple of little signs and road names that suggest it was ever there. Another lasted at Alexandra Park in north London, just beneath the palace, until 1970. A few are still used for point-to-points and others, such as the remaining grandstand at defunct Lincoln, are just a memory of the past.

Thankfully there are still tracks across the country and it is the ambition of many a keen racegoer to tick them all off their list. None are without their charm, from Ffos Las in far west Wales, landscaped and opened on the site of an old colliery in 2009, to Cartmel, in chocolate box Lake District countryside in a land where time seems to stand still. A few on the coming pages are world-famous and are must-sees to see for anyone interested in the sport.

Aintree

Set in a grey, suburban landscape on the outskirts of Liverpool, Aintree is not the prettiest of racecourses. Its future was even in jeopardy over a possible land sale, before a public funding campaign saw it saved by Jockey Club Racecourses in 1983. It has been the setting for the world's most famous horse race since the 1830s and comes alive in early April for the three-day Grand National meeting. The national is the people's race and draws spectators from across the region, with many ignoring the occasional bad weather to dress in their finest for Ladies' Day. More than 150,000 visit across the three days leading up to the big race itself on a Saturday. The track is easy to get to by road and local rail and holds other meetings in the winter and spring.

Major dates: Grand National meeting (April)

▼ Aintree racecourse, the home of the Grand National

Ascot

The grandest of all racing stages, particularly with the pomp, ceremony and world-class Flat racing associated with Royal Ascot. It was founded by Queen Anne in 1711 and is protected by an Act of Parliament. Modern-day Ascot probably looks very different, especially since it was reopened after a £200 million redevelopment in 2006. While the facilities and services are modern, it somehow retains a sense of history and tradition. Whether or not you go to the Royal meeting, you will see top-class horses and jockeys. Ascot is far more famous for its Flat racing, also hosting the end-of-season British Champions Day, but it holds meetings year-round and has some high-quality jumping in the winter.

Major dates: Royal Ascot (late June), King George VI & Queen Elizabeth Stakes (late July), British Champions Day (late October), Clarence House Chase (late January)

▲ Ascot has no rival for pageantry and tradition

Cheltenham

It is not overstating it to describe Cheltenham as jump racing's Mecca. Weeks of build-up lead to the four days of the Cheltenham Festival in the spring, and a spine-tingling roar from the crowd when the first race is off. It is where champions are crowned in the Gold Cup and Champion Hurdle, millions of pounds are wagered and pints of Guinness are drunk. It is also located in the most stunning setting, surrounded by steep Cotswold hills, and has carefully moved with the times with its ever-changing infrastructure managing to seamlessly metamorphose into

▼ The Cheltenham Festival every March is top of every jumps fan's agenda

the future, while managing to remain the Cheltenham the fans hold dear.

Any day's racing at Cheltenham is worth a visit, with most of those that will eventually run at the Festival appearing at the other earlier meetings during the winter, just without the same stifling numbers of spectators.

Major dates: Festival Trials Day (late January), Cheltenham Festival (mid-March), November Meeting (mid-November)

Epsom

Part of the rolling North Downs, just outside London, Epsom is home to the most historic Flat race, the Derby. It was created in 1779 when the Earl of Derby won a coin toss against Sir Charles Bunbury as to the naming of a new race. This mile-and-a-half event for three-year-old colts developed into the most important of its kind and very few winners of it are not considered champions and future stallions. The track's extraordinary turns and cambers test every inch of a young horse, and many are not suited to it.

The Derby was moved from a Wednesday to a Saturday in 1995 and has always attracted a huge crowd, with open-top buses lining the home straight. The Oaks, the equivalent of the Derby for fillies, is run the day before. While other meetings draw a fraction of the attendance, Epsom is populated all year round by a few trainers, and early risers will see horses making their way out to the gallops in the middle of the racecourse for their morning exercise.

Major dates: Derby Festival (early June)

▲ Epsom racecourse is an undulating and difficult test for a horse

▼ Epsom town sign

Goodwood

One of the definite contenders for the title of most beautiful racecourse in the world, Goodwood provides stunning views of the West Sussex countryside, and even the English Channel, from its position perched on the South Downs. While

▼ Even the great Bing Crosby has been to Goodwood

Bing Crosby receiving from Mrs Ann Barnes the trophy for the 1975 PTS Laurels on behalf of Mr D. Galbraith, the owner of Hail the Pirates.

▲ There is no more pleasant a place to be than Goodwood on a warm day

Glorious Goodwood, the annual highlight, is not as well-known internationally as Royal Ascot, it has its own tradition more akin to a smart garden party. The five-day meeting attracts the best Flat horses but it is a different test to Ascot, being severely undulating. Goodwood is part of the Duke of Richmond's estate, which includes a fine country house and vintage motor circuit. It holds Flat racing through the summer months but its exposed hilltop setting means it is best enjoyed on a sunny day.

Major dates: Glorious Goodwood (late July/early August)

York

Proud Yorkshire folk would recoil at the suggestion that York is the Ascot of the north, but it is such a near equivalent that Royal Ascot was moved there in 2005 when its usual home was being redeveloped. Similarly flat and with a proud tradition, it is another racecourse that provides a very classy day out. It was once a swampy area of land just outside the city walls known as the Knavesmire, still an alternative name for the track today, and was the site of the hanging of highwayman Dick Turpin in 1739.

Flat racing has been held at York since those times, although it has been quietly but tastefully modernised since then. The Ebor meeting, for four days during the summer, is one of Europe's most important festivals, from both a racing and a social aspect.

Major dates: Dante meeting (mid-May), Ebor meeting (mid-August)

The National Heritage Centre

Newmarket's racing museum was completely relocated and designed into a heritage centre as part of a huge project that was completed in 2016 and began to win awards almost immediately.

It serves not only as the perfect introduction to the sport for the young and the uninitiated, but also provides reams of new information for the most knowledgeable racing fan. Situated on (and just behind) the High Street in Newmarket, the National Heritage Centre was developed on the site of what was once a palace for King Charles II.

Palace House, a fine red-brick listed building built on remnants of the palace, had fallen into disrepair but has been restored into a gallery of sporting art, with paintings of racing

▲ The National Horseracing Museum has a range of interactive displays to entertain all ages

and other country pursuits going back to the 17th century through the contemporary exhibitions. Two historic stables have also been converted into attractions. The King's Yard became the National Horseracing Museum, packed full of ancient documents and collections as well as audio-visual and interactive displays.

Another part of the site, the Rothschild Yard, has become something of a living museum. Retired racehorses, some of whom were very accomplished, live in the boxes and gladly receive visitors. The Retraining of Racehorses charity arranges several demonstrations with them during the day.

◀ Historic Palace House has been restored to its former glory and now houses an art collection

▼ Some exhibits at the National Heritage Centre are allowed to be touched! *(Mark Atkins)*

Racing in Ireland

Going racing in Ireland is an almost identical experience to Britain, with very similar rules, terminology and betting. The two jurisdictions are very closely linked with horses regularly moving in between, either permanently, or just for a race on one day. Ireland is the biggest breeder of Thoroughbreds in Europe. It has such a competitive domestic racing scene that many jockeys decide to up sticks and move across the Irish Sea in search of easier pickings.

There are 26 racecourses, two of which are in Northern Ireland, and come in just as wide a variety as Britain, both in terms of topography and of the type of races they hold. The most iconic is Laytown in County Meath, which has just one meeting on a beach every September.

Trainers are located across the country with the only major cluster of stables being at The Curragh in County Kildare, where around 1,000 horses are trained by 60 licence holders and there are 1,500 acres of ancient land on which to exercise them. The Curragh is also the premier Irish Flat racecourse, an Irish version of Newmarket: a largely flat expanse of green that it is not the

easiest place to get to but always stages top-quality racing. All five of the Irish Classics are held at The Curragh and it is also home to The Turf Club, Irish racing's regulatory body.

Leopardstown is the country's major metropolitan racecourse. Situated on the outskirts of Dublin, it is very accessible and offers fine viewing facilities, with excellent Flat and jump racing throughout the year. The highlights are two jumps festivals just after Christmas and in early February and the Irish Champion Stakes, Ireland's biggest Flat race, in the autumn.

Whilst Saturday is the showcase day in Britain, in Ireland it is usually Sunday. With televised coverage widely shared, racing enthusiasts are able to follow both scenes closely and, for the jumps, are up to speed on all the form when the cream of their divisions meet at the Cheltenham Festival. Irish racecards are also published in British editions of the *Racing Post*.

Any day's racing in Ireland is perhaps a little more relaxed than Britain, with no enforced dress code. Facilities at most racecourses are more rudimentary, so being prepared for the weather is the biggest priority. There is racing most days, if not every day, and the so-called 'festival' meetings are the greatest attraction. They vary from Killarney, a contender for the world's

▼ Racing on the beach at Laytown, which takes place just one day a year, is one of Irish sport's most incredible spectacles

most beautiful racecourse, through to the top-class jumping at Punchestown. Then there is Galway, lasting seven days through the summer with off-track entertainment stretching into the small hours of the night. Irish racegoers tend to be very well informed, so even if you have no ideas of your own there will be no shortage of people happy to give you a tip.

Major dates: Punchestown Festival (Jumps), Punchestown County Meath (late April/early May), Irish Derby (Flat), Curragh, County Kildare (late June/early July), Galway Festival (Mixed), Galway (late July/early August), Irish Champion Stakes (Flat), Leopardstown, Dublin (September)

▲ Racing over the banks fences at the Punchestown Festival in the spring

Visit: Irish National Stud

Close to The Curragh in racing's heartland, the public can visit what is still an active and important stud with more than a century of history. The Irish National Stud, which has a number of stallions and offers services such as foaling and looking after young horse for breeders, allows impressive access behind the scenes. It also counts among its residents some retired champion racehorses, its 'Living Legends', who can be viewed in the fields and stables. There is a horse museum that exhibits the skeleton of the unparalleled jumper Arkle among its artefacts and memorabilia. Entrance also includes the world-renowned Japanese Gardens and the more recent St Fiachra's Garden, which attempts to evoke ancient Ireland.

◄ The Irish National Stud *(Irish National Stud)*

▼ Feeding time for the 'Living Legends' at the Irish National Stud

Racing in France

From the chic Normandy seaside resort of Deauville to the grand old racecourses of Paris, there is a lot of style about a visit to the races in France. Both Flat and jump racing can be found through most of the year in what is essentially a tiered system. The top-quality action is nearly all based around the capital and most of the best horses are trained at nearby Chantilly.

During the week, there are usually only a couple of meetings per day. One will be around Paris, with the other in one of the regions. Do not be surprised to turn up at one of the Parisian venues to find it completely deserted; aside from a few major occasions, they nearly always are. On Saturdays and Sundays, there are race meetings all over the country, some of which are at small and very obscure venues that are more akin to a British point-to-point meeting. Details of all can be found under the governing body's website: www.france-galop.com.

Lack of attendance at the big tracks is particularly baffling because most are easily accessible by public transport and cost of entrance is, if not free, then virtually nominal. One major reason for this is that there are no private bookmakers and all betting is of the pool variety under the state-operated Pari Mutuel Urbain (PMU). Plenty of this is funnelled back in to fund the handsome prize money and maintain the racecourses and training grounds.

Also, there are PMU machines or offices in bars and cafes in most French towns, so punters can watch from there rather than go to the track. It makes for a strange atmosphere, and such silence that you can often hear the jockeys shouting as they fight out the finish of a race. Free form sheets are handed out at the entrance, but for a more detailed guide, an enthusiast or 'turfiste' will opt for the French racing daily newspaper *Paris Turf*.

Longchamp, which provides a clear view of the Eiffel Tower and is in the middle of the Bois de Boulogne park to the west of Paris and near the Roland-Garros tennis centre, is home to many of France's biggest Flat meetings but principally the Prix de l'Arc de Triomphe. This is the final and perhaps greatest test of the best European horses in the Flat season calendar, over the same Derby distance of a mile and a half. French-based horses regularly win important races around the world, but the 'Arc' is the one that all of their trainers most want to win.

Jumping is not generally as popular in France as Flat or trotting races. Another grand Parisian track, Auteuil, holds nearly all of the important races including an equivalent to the Gold Cup and Champion Hurdle. Most of these are in the spring and early summer, over a formidable set of brush fences.

It is easy enough to place bets in France with basic French, certainly for win (gagnant) and place (placé), with variously more complicated couplé (exacta) and trios. Every day there is a big handicap race, called the Tiercé, which has a big field to stimulate betting.

Major dates: Grand Steeple-Chase de Paris (French Gold Cup), Auteil (late May), Prix du Jockey Club (French Derby), Chantilly (early June), Deauville Races (August), Prix de l'Arc de Triomphe, Longchamp (first Sunday in October)

Visit: Chantilly

Chantilly's racecourse is one of the finest in the world, with elegant grandstands and top-quality racing and it is overlooked by a huge chateau and even more magnificent 18th-century stables. The chateau contains the Musée Condé, full of priceless artwork and an extraordinary library full of rare manuscripts, while the stables, or Grandes Écuries, is a museum of the horse.

The place has as rich a history as the sport has in Britain but as interesting as visiting any of those attractions is to see the working life of the 2,500 or so racehorses who are based at France's training headquarters. Morning exercise takes place on tree-lined tracks in the forest, which open up into a huge open expanse of grassland known as 'Les Aigles'. Many of France's star horses can be seen here. Chantilly is also easy to reach by road or rail, being only half an hour north of the capital.

▼ Longchamp, close to the centre of Paris, is France's premier racecourse

Racing in Europe

It might be surprising to learn that racecourses can be found in most European countries and that even seemingly unlikely destinations such as Norway, Cyprus and Romania are affiliates of the International Federation Of Horseracing Authorities, which promotes best practice and harmonisation of rules. However, it is not always easy to find out about fixtures outside using local media.

In most of these places racing is considered a minority sport at best and is often competing, as is most notable across Scandinavia, with trotting. The most notable exceptions are Germany and Italy, which hold mostly Flat racing, but occasional jumping too. German racing has undergone a resurgence in recent years, largely through better organisation and funding, and its domestic-bred horses, renowned for their durability, have become popular around Europe. There is good-quality racing throughout the year and you can find a track at most of the major cities. The social highlight is the week-long late summer festival at the spa town of Baden-Baden.

Italian racing, meanwhile, has taken a dip in fortunes. The home of such greats as jockey Frankie Dettori and Ribot, champion horse of Europe in the mid-1950s, it has suffered

▲ Meetings are regularly held in Sweden at Stockholm's new Bro Park Racecourse *(Swedish Horseracing Authority)*

from political in-fighting, poor management and even strikes. Nonetheless, it continues, and the grand old racecourses of Capannelle in Rome and San Siro in Milan are well worth a look if in the area on the right weekend.

One curiosity that attracts many racing tourists – and the odd equestrian participant – from Britain and Ireland is the Velka Pardubicka at Pardubice, about an hour west of Prague in the Czech Republic. This is perhaps the most formidable jumps race in the world, taking in a variety of obstacles, sections over a ploughed field, and a distance of more than four miles. For a century and a half, the challenge has attracted international riders and remains a tremendous viewing spectacle even if, thankfully, it has been made safer for the welfare of horse and rider.

Major dates: Derby Italiano, Capannelle, Rome (May), Deutsches Derby, Hamburg (July), Grosser Preis von Baden, Baden-Baden (early September), Velka Pardubicka, Czech Republic (second Sunday in October)

Racing in America

The principal rules are the same, they are still Thoroughbred horses and it is a matter of the best one on the day passing the post first, but there are a number of differences to be experienced going racing in America.

For a start, the tracks are nearly uniform in dimension, with a dirt oval of around a mile in circumference hosting the majority of races. Only some important ones have a grass course, either inside or outside the dirt oval, which are used less frequently. Many courses also double up as casinos, sometimes leading to a strange experience when you find a decent crowd there, but with very few people actually watching the racing.

While the sport has declined in popularity since the glamour days up to the 1960s, it still has dates fixed in the American psyche. The Triple Crown, a series of three races in the spring starting with the Kentucky Derby, gains national coverage and six-figure crowds. Very few three-year-old colts complete the hat-trick of Kentucky Derby, Preakness Stakes and Belmont Stakes, which are held within a few weeks of each other. American Pharoah ended a 37-year wait for a champion in 2015.

In such a large country, there are regional rather than national championships for jockeys and trainers. As opposed to Europe, where a racecourse's meetings are spread out, American tracks tend to have intense seasons lasting a few weeks before the travelling circus moves elsewhere. Competition is fiercest in California and New York, while the home of breeding, administration and the racecourses of Churchill Downs and Keeneland are all based in Kentucky. Saratoga, a spa town in New York State, is home to the National Museum of Racing and Hall of Fame as well as a major racing season in August. Del Mar racecourse, on the Californian coast close to San Diego, is the other summer spot on any fan's to-do list.

The majority of gambling is via a state-run pool style, and in some states this is the only way you can have a bet. Punters (confusingly referred to in the US as 'handicappers') take quite a sophisticated approach as form guides have far more information on timing and even publish the weights of horses. It is possible to do simple win bets, but it seems more popular to place more complicated combination and jackpot-style wagers.

Major dates: Kentucky Derby, Churchill Downs, Kentucky (first Saturday in May), Preakness Stakes, Pimlico, Baltimore (mid-May), Belmont Stakes, Belmont Park, New York (early June), Breeders' Cup, various (early November)

▼ A big crowd attends the Fall Meet at Keeneland in Kentucky each autumn *(Keeneland photo)*

Racing in the rest of the world

Racing is a huge business in Asia. Japanese racing regularly draws enormous crowds – Tokyo's main racecourse has a capacity of more than 200,000 – and particular horses have a devoted following. Through careful importation of top-class stallions and mares from Europe and America, its breeding industry is now among the best in the world and Japanese horses have regularly tasted success overseas.

Hong Kong, where the British introduced racing in the mid-1800s, also has a fanatical fan base. Its two tracks race once a week each, with lucrative prizes attracting top global jockeys through the winter, while high-quality horses are purchased from Europe at great expense to race there. Gambling is such a popular pursuit that betting turnover per race is the highest in the world.

The passion for racing is very different in Dubai, with the scene's development driven by its ruler Sheikh Mohammed. Although there has long been a traditional interest in the native Arabian horse, the first Flat Thoroughbred meeting was not held until 1981, on an old camel track. Rapidly, the Maktoum family has created a handful of racecourses and training areas

from out of the desert with the jewel in the crown being the colossal construction of Meydan, with its grandstand stretching for a mile. Prize money is such that the January to March season attracts a host of international raiders, culminating in the Dubai World Cup, for some time now the most valuable race in the world.

The sport is also a regularly enjoyed pastime in Australia and New Zealand, where there are meetings every day, mostly Flat racing on turf with occasional jump racing. The Australian breeding industry is similarly flourishing and its sprinters, exemplified by the brilliant unbeaten mare Black Caviar who came to Royal Ascot in 2012, are considered the world's best. The whole of Australia stops for the first Tuesday in November, which becomes a bank holiday for the Melbourne Cup. This 24-runner handicap, over two miles of Flemington racecourse, attracts the cream of the world's staying horses and is part of a week-long meeting which ranks at the top of the Australian social calendar.

Major dates: Dubai World Cup, Meydan (late March), Melbourne Cup, Flemington (first Tuesday in November), Japan Cup, Tokyo (last Sunday of November), Hong Kong International Races, Sha Tin (mid-December)

▼ Horses exercise in front of the enormous Meydan grandstand in the early hours of the morning *(Mathea Kelley/Dubai Racing Club)*

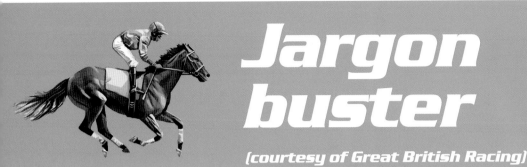

Jargon buster

(courtesy of Great British Racing)

Accumulator A bet involving more than one horse/race. Each winning selection then goes on to the next horse (bet). All selections must be successful to win any money back.

Act (on the ground/on the track etc) Describes a horse's suitability or previous ability for different conditions e.g. going, racecourses etc.

Age All Thoroughbreds have their birthdays on 1 January.

Allowance Inexperienced riders (apprentices, conditionals and amateurs) are allowed a weight concession to compensate for their lack of experience against their colleagues. The 'allowance' is usually 3lb, 5lb or 7lb, with it decreasing as the young jockey rides more winners.

All-weather tracks (AWT) Racing on an artificial surface.

Amateur A non-professional jockey who does not receive a fee for riding in a race, denoted on the racecard by the prefix Mr, Mrs, Miss, Captain, etc. Some races are restricted to amateurs.

Ante-post For many major races such as the Grand National, you can place your bet well in advance of the day. The price of the horse is usually bigger than you would expect to see on the day as it reflects the fact that it is not guaranteed to line up in the race.

Apprentice A trainee Flat jockey connected to the stable of a licensed trainer. Apprentices have a weight allowance when they ride in races against professional jockeys.

At the post When all the horses have arrived at the start before a race, they are said to be 'at the post'.

Auction maiden For two-year-olds sold at public auction as yearlings or two-year-olds, for a price not exceeding a specified figure.

Breeze-up Type of auction, usually for two-year-olds, at which the horses for sale run for a short distance to allow prospective buyers to assess them.

Bridle The equipment on a horse's head used to control it.

Bridle, won on the Won easily, without being hard ridden or challenged by other horses.

Broke down When a horse sustains an injury during a race.

Broodmare Mare kept for breeding purposes.

Brought down A horse that falls during a race when impeded by another horse.

Bumper A Flat race run under jump rules, used to educate young horses before they tackle hurdles or fences. Officially called National Hunt Flat races.

Bit Metal part of the bridle that sits in a horse's mouth. The reins are then attached to the bit and used by the jockey to control the horse.

Black type Term used by the bloodstock industry to denote a horse that has won or been placed in a Pattern/Listed race. Horses 'going for black type' are attempting to win or be placed in a Pattern/Listed race to improve their breeding value.

Blanket finish When the horses finish so close together at the winning line you could theoretically put a single blanket across them.

Bleeder A horse that tends to break blood vessels during a race.

Blinkers/blinds A form of headgear worn by the horse, consisting of a hood with cups around the eyes. They limit a horse's vision and reduce distractions to make it concentrate. A horse wearing blinkers is denoted on a racecard by a small 'b' next to its weight.

Book A record of the bets made on a particular race or other sporting event. A bookmaker 'makes a book' by determining the likelihood of each possible outcome in a race and presenting this in the form of odds. The book is adjusted according to the amount of money and bets struck on each possible outcome.

Bookmaker/bookie A person/company licensed to accept bets.

Boxwalker A horse that constantly walks around its stable and doesn't settle.

Break (a horse) in Teaching a young horse to accept riding equipment and carry a rider.

Breeder Someone that breeds racehorses. They own the dam (mother) at the time the foal is born.

Backed A 'backed' horse is one upon which lots of money has been placed, and its odds have decreased.

Backward A horse that is either too young or not fully fit.

Banker The horse expected to win – usually a short-priced favourite. The strongest selection in a multiple selection.

Bar Term used when describing bookmakers' prices, e.g., '4-1 bar two' means that you can obtain at least 4-1 about any horse except for the first two in the betting.

Bay Horse colour – any brown horse with a black mane/tail and legs.

Betting market A market is created, according to demand, by the prices offered for each runner by bookmakers.

Betting ring The main area at a racecourse where the bookmakers operate.

Colours Jacket ('silks') worn by a jockey to identify a horse. A horse runs in its owner's registered colour combination.

Colt Ungelded (entire) male horse below five years of age.

Conditional jockey A jump jockey, under 26, who receives a weight allowance for inexperience until they have ridden a certain number of winners.

Conditions race A race in which horses are allotted extra weight according to factors including sex, age, whether they are a previous winner, etc. This is a better-class race for horses just below Group or Listed level.

Conformation A horse's build and general physical structure.

Connections People associated with a horse, such as the owner and trainer.

Covered up When a jockey keeps a horse behind other runners to prevent it running too freely in the early stages of a race.

Covering The mating of horses.

Cut in the ground A description of softer ground conditions.

Co-favourite A horse that shares its position at the head of the betting market with at least two other horses.

Chaser A horse that takes part in steeplechase races.

Cheekpieces Strips of sheepskin that are attached to the side of a horse's bridle, partially obscuring its rear vision so that it concentrates. Horses wearing cheekpieces are denoted on a racecard by a small 'p'.

Chestnut Horse colour varying from light, washy yellow to dark liver orange.

Claimer (jockey) An apprentice Flat jockey.

Claiming race/Claimer A race in which each horse's weight is determined by the price placed on them by connections. The lower the claiming price, the lower the weight. Horses can be 'claimed' (bought) for the specified price after the race.

Classic Group of historic major races for three-year-olds in the Flat season. These are the 2000 Guineas, the 1000 Guineas, the Oaks, the Derby and the St Leger.

Clerk of the course Racecourse official responsible for the overall racecourse management, including the preparation of the racing surface.

Clerk of the scales Racecourse official whose chief duty is to weigh the riders before and after a race to ensure proper weight is carried.

Distance The margin by which a horse has won or has been beaten (in lengths). In jump racing, if a horse is beaten/wins by a long way (more than 30 lengths) it is said to have been beaten/won by a distance.

Dividend The amount that a winning or placed horse returns for every £1 bet.

Double Consists of one bet involving two selections in different events. Both selections must be successful to get a return, with the winnings from the first selection going on to the second selection.

Draw A horse's starting position in the stalls allotted in races on the Flat. A horse with a seemingly advantageous draw is said to be 'well drawn'.

Drifter A horse whose odds get bigger just before the race due to a lack of support in the market. Often referred to as being 'on the drift'.

Dam A horse's mother.

Damsire (broodmare) The sire of a broodmare; in human terms, the maternal grandfather of a horse.

Dark horse A horse regarded as having potential but whose full capabilities have not been revealed.

Dead-heat A tie between two or more horses for first place, or for one of the other finishing positions. In the event of a dead-heat for first place, when a winning bet has been made, half the stake is applied to the selection at full odds and the other half is lost.

Decimal odds Used on the Tote and betting exchanges, instead of fractional odds. Decimal odds are expressed as a figure (in round or decimal terms) that represents the potential total winning return to the punter. So, 4 (or 4.0) in Tote or decimal odds is the same as the conventional 3-1, as it represents a potential total winning return of £4 to a £1 stake.

Declared (runner) A horse confirmed to start in a race at the final declarations stage.

Each-way A bet where half the total stake is for the selection to win and half is for the selection to be placed.

Enquiry – stewards' enquiry Review of the race to check into a possible infraction of the rules made by the stewards. If the enquiry could affect the result of the race, an announcement will be made on course.

Entire horse An ungelded horse.

Evens/Even money A price of 1-1. When your stake brings equal winnings e.g. £10 staked at evens wins £10 (total return £20).

Exacta/Straight forecast A bet picking the first and second in a race in the exact order of finish.

Flat racing Racing without jumps.

Foal A horse from birth to 1 January of the following year (when it becomes a yearling).

Forecast A bet where the aim is to select both the winner and runner-up in a race. A straight forecast is the winner and runner-up in the correct order. A dual or reverse forecast is the winner and runner-up in either order.

Form A horse's race record denoted by figures (and letters) next to its name on a racecard. The form figures are read backwards from right to left.

Furlong 220 yards (one eighth of a mile). The numbered posts on British racecourses count the furlongs back from the winning post.

Fancied When a horse is expected to win or at least to be involved in the finish.

Favourite The horse with the shortest odds in the race.

Field The number of horses in a race or, in betting, all of the horses in a race except the favourite.

Filly Female horse aged four years old or younger.

Group/Graded races These races form the upper tier of the racing structure, with Group/Grade 1 the most important, followed by Group/Grade 2 and Group/Grade 3. Group races are run on the Flat; Graded races are run over jumps (the most important Flat races in the United States are also Graded).

Guineas (currency) A guinea was one pound and one shilling (£1.05 in decimal currency) and, traditionally, the prices of horses sold at public auction were given in guineas.

Guineas (race) Shorthand for the 1000 Guineas and/or 2000 Guineas.

Gallops Training ground where horses are exercised.

Gelding A male horse that has been castrated.

Get the trip To stay the distance.

Going The condition of the racing surface. Ranges from heavy to firm.

Going down When horses are on their way to the start.

Green Used to describe an immature or inexperienced horse.

Half-brother/sister When two horses have the same mother (dam), they are half-brothers/sisters. Horses are not referred to as half-brothers/sisters when they share only the same father (sire).

Handicap A race where each horse is allotted a different weight to carry, according to the official ratings determined by the official handicappers. The theory is that all horses run on a fair and equal basis – the 'perfect' handicap being one where all the runners finish in a dead-heat.

Handicap mark/Rating

Each horse, once it has run a few times (usually three), is allocated an official handicap rating, which is used to determine its weight if it runs in a handicap. If a horse does well, its handicap rating will go up; if it performs poorly, its rating will go down.

Hard ridden Used to describe a horse whose jockey is expending full effort on the horse, and using their whip.

Hurdles The smaller obstacles on a jumps course. Horses usually have a season or two over hurdles before progressing to fences, though some continue to specialise in hurdling.

In-running betting Betting on the outcome of a race during the race itself, rather than beforehand. In-running odds can change rapidly as the race unfolds.

Juvenile A two-year-old horse on the Flat.

Juvenile hurdler The youngest category of hurdler – those that turn four years of age (on 1 January) during the season in which they start hurdling.

Jackpot The Jackpot is a Tote bet that requires the selection of the winners of the first six races at a selected meeting.

Jocked off Term used to refer to when one jockey is replaced by another on a horse they usually ride or has already been booked to ride in a particular race.

Joint-favourite If two horses have the shortest odds in the betting, they are described as joint-favourites.

Judge Racecourse official responsible for declaring the finishing order of a race and the distances between the runners.

Lay To take a bet on: a bookmaker's offer quoting the price at which he wishes to trade. 'I'll lay 6-4 this favourite.' Betting on a horse to lose.

Layer An alternative term for a bookmaker, someone who lays or accepts a bet.

Left-handed track Racecourse where horses run anti-clockwise.

Length A unit of measurement for the distances between each horse at the finish of a race; the measurement of a horse from head to tail.

Level weights When all horses are carrying the same weight. These are usually major races.

Listed race A class of race just below a Group or Graded quality.

Levy A surcharge collected from bookmakers, based on their turnover or gross profits, which goes towards prize money, improvements to racecourses, and other areas such as scientific research.

Longshot A horse with high odds (an outsider).

Maiden A horse that has yet to win a race.

Mare Female horse aged five years old or above.

Median auction maiden A race for two-year-olds by stallions that had one or more yearling sold in the previous year with a median price not exceeding a specified figure.

Middle distances On the Flat, races beyond a mile and up to 1m 6f are the middle distances.

Minimum trip The shortest race distance: five furlongs on the Flat, two miles over jumps.

Neck Unit of measurement in a race finish about the length of a horse's neck.

Non-runner A horse that was originally meant to run but for some reason has been withdrawn from the race.

Nose Smallest official distance a horse can win by.

Non-trier A horse that is prevented by the jockey from running to its full ability. Non-trying is a serious offence.

Novice A horse in the early stages of its career after it has won its first race.

Novice auction A race for novices sold at public auction as yearlings or two-year-olds for a price not exceeding a specified figure.

Novice stakes A Flat race for two-year-olds or three-year-olds that have not won more than twice.

Nursery A handicap on the Flat for two-year-old horses.

Nap The best bet of the day from a particular tipster.

National Hunt Racing over fences and hurdles; informally referred to as jump racing.

Outsider Long-priced horse in the betting, regarded as unlikely to win.

Over the top When a horse is considered to be past its peak due to too much racing/training and needs a rest.

Overweight When a horse carries more than its allocated weight, due to the jockey being unable to make that weight.

Objection A complaint by one jockey against another regarding the running of a race.

Odds The chance offered for a selection to win. Also known as price.

Odds-against

Betting odds where the potential winnings are higher than the stake. The numerator is larger than the denominator (e.g. 2-1).

Odds-on Betting odds where the stake is higher than the potential winnings if the bet is successful. The denominator is larger than the numerator (e.g. 1-2).

Off the bridle Describes a horse being pushed along and losing contact with the bit in its mouth.

One-paced Describes a horse that is unable to raise its pace in the closing stages of a race.

On the bridle Describes a horse running comfortably, still having a bite on the bit. A horse that wins 'on the bridle' is regarded as having won easily.

On the nose (to bet) Placing a win bet.

Open ditch Steeplechase jump with a ditch on the approach side to the fence.

Out of the handicap When handicap races are framed, there is a maximum and minimum weight that horses can carry. When a horse's rating means that its allocated weight is lower than the minimum for that race, it is said to be 'out of the handicap'.

Out of the money A horse that finishes outside of the place money.

Pacemaker A horse that is entered in a race with the intention that it will set the pace for another horse with the same connections.

Paddock Area of the racecourse incorporating the parade ring (where horses are paraded prior to the race) and winners' enclosure.

Parade Before major races, the horses often line up in racecard order (numerical order) and are led in front of the grandstands to allow racegoers to see them.

Patent Multiple bet consisting of seven bets involving three selections in different events. A single on each selection, plus three doubles and one treble. One successful selection guarantees a return.

Pattern The grading system for the most important races.

Penalty Additional weight carried by a horse on account of previous wins.

Photo finish In a close race, where the placings cannot be determined easily, the result is determined by the judge by examination of a photograph taken by a camera on the finishing line.

Placepot Similar rules to the Jackpot, but your selections have only to be placed.

Pulled up A horse that drops out of a race and does not finish.

Pulling When a horse is unsettled during the early part of a race and uses too much energy, fighting the jockey by pulling against the bridle.

Punter A person who gambles.

Pushed out When a horse is ridden vigorously, but without full effort by the jockey.

Quarters The hind parts of a horse, specifically between flank and tail.

Rails (racecourse) White plastic rails used to mark out the track on a racecourse. The stands rails are those nearest the grandstand and the far rails are those on the opposite side of the track from the grandstand.

Rails (betting) Bookmakers are not allowed in the members' area, but some bookmakers are allowed to set up their pitches on the side of the rails, allowing them to accept bets. Rails bookmakers are the top end of the racecourse betting market, usually dealing with credit customers.

Rating A measure of the ability of a horse on a scale starting at zero and going into three figures. Flat and jump racing use different scales; the highest-rated Flat horse is usually in the 130s and the top-rated jumper in the 180s.

Right-handed track Racecourse where horses run clockwise.

Rule 4 deduction One of the most commonly invoked betting rules, dealing with deductions from winning bets in the event of any late withdrawn runners from a race. When there is insufficient time to reform the betting market, a rate of deductions is in proportion to the odds of the non-runner(s) at the time of withdrawal.

Sprint races Flat races run over a distance of five or six furlongs.

Stallion Male breeding horse.

Stalls handler Member of a team employed to load horses into the stalls for Flat races and to move the stalls to the correct position for the start of each race.

Starter Racecourse official responsible for starting a horse race.

Starting price Often abbreviated to SP. The starting prices are the final odds prevailing at the time the race starts and are used to determine the payout to winning punters, unless a punter took a specified price at the time of placing the bet.

Stayer A horse that specialises in racing over long distances (two miles and above) on the Flat.

Staying chaser A horse that races over three miles or more over fences.

Steeplechasing A race over fences, open ditches and water jumps, run over distances from two miles up to four and a half miles.

Steward One of the officials in overall charge of a race meeting, including disciplinary procedures.

Stewards' enquiry A hearing held by the stewards into a race to determine whether the rules of racing have been broken.

Stick A jockey's whip

String All the horses in a particular training stable.

Stud A farm where horses are mated. Usually home to one or more stallions.

Supplementary entry Major races such as the Derby have an early initial entry date and several forfeit stages. A supplementary entry can be made in the week leading up to the race, subject to a substantial fee.

Schooling Training a horse for jumping.

Second string The stable's second choice from two or more runners in a race.

Selling plate/selling race Low-class race in which the winner is offered at auction afterwards; other horses in the race may be claimed for a fixed sum. If the winning stable buys back its own horse it is said to be 'bought in'. The racecourse receives a percentage of the selling price of each horse.

Short price Low odds, meaning a punter will get little return for their initial outlay.

Silks See 'Colours'.

Silver ring A racecourse enclosure, usually the one with the lowest admission price.

Sire Father of a horse.

Spread a plate When a horse damages or loses a horseshoe before a race, it is said to have 'spread a plate'. The horse has to be re-shod by a farrier, often delaying the start of the race.

Springer A horse whose price shortens dramatically.

Tattersalls (racecourse enclosure) The enclosure next in status to the members'. Those choosing this enclosure have access to the main betting area and the paddock.

Thoroughbred A breed of horse used for racing.

Tongue tie Strip of material tied around a horse's tongue and lower jaw to keep it from swallowing its tongue, which can clog its air passage. A horse wearing a tongue tie is denoted on a racecard by a small 't' next to the horse's weight.

Tote (betting) Pool betting on racecourses. All the stakes on a particular bet are pooled, before a deduction is made to cover the Tote's costs and contribution to racing. The remainder of the pool is divided by the number of winning units to give a dividend that is declared inclusive of a £1 stake. Odds fluctuate according to the pattern of betting and betting ceases when the race starts.

Trainer The person responsible for looking after a horse and preparing it to race.

Treble A three-leg accumulator. All three selections must be successful to get a return; the winnings from the first selection automatically go on to the second and then on to the third.

Trip Another term for the distance of a race. When a horse has the stamina for a certain distance, it is said to 'stay/get the trip'.

Triple Crown In Britain, for colts the Triple Crown comprises the 2000 Guineas, the Derby and the St Leger; for fillies, the 1000 Guineas, the Oaks and the St Leger. Winning all three races is a rare feat. The American Triple Crown comprises the Kentucky Derby, Preakness Stakes and Belmont Stakes.

Trixie Multiple bet consisting of four bets involving three selections in different events. The bet includes three doubles and one treble. A minimum of two selections must be successful to get a return.

Turned out Racecourses often have a 'best turned out' award for the horse judged to have been best presented in the paddock.

Turn of foot A horse's ability to accelerate in the closing stages of a race.

Under starters orders/under orders The moment a race is about to begin. Once the horses are in the stalls for a Flat race, or have lined up at the start for a jumps race, they are said to be 'under starter's orders' as the jockeys are waiting for the starter's signal to begin the race.

Unfancied Not expected to win.

Valet A person employed to prepare a jockey's equipment in the weighing room.

Visor Similar to blinkers, but with a slit in each eye cup to allow some lateral vision. A horse wearing a visor is denoted on a racecard by a small 'v' next to the horse's weight.

Weighing in/out Each jockey (wearing racing kit and carrying their saddle) must stand on the scales before and after the race, so that it can be checked that they are carrying the correct weight allotted to their horse. When the weights carried by the winner and placed horses have been verified after the race, there will be an announcement that they have 'weighed in'. This confirms the race result and at this point bookmakers will pay out on successful bets.

Weight cloth A cloth with pockets for lead weights placed under the saddle to ensure that a horse carries its allotted weight.

Weight for age A graduated scale that shows how horses of differing ages progress month by month during the racing season, the differences being expressed in terms of weight. This allows horses of differing ages to compete against each other on a fair basis, based on their age and maturity, in what are known as weight-for-age races.

Weights Lead placed in a weight cloth. When these weights are added to the jockey's weight and other equipment, the total weight should equal the weight allotted to the jockey's horse in a race.

Well in When a horse is considered to be favoured by the weights in a race, it is said to be 'well in'.

Win bet/only
A single bet on a horse to finish first. Win only markets signify that no each-way betting is available.

Whip
Or stick. Used by jockey as an aid to encourage or steer and balance the horse.

Work rider A stable employee, not necessarily a licensed jockey, who rides horses in training on the gallops.

Walkover A race involving only one horse. The horse and its jockey must pass the winning post to be declared the winner.

Yankee Multiple bet consisting of 11 bets (six doubles, four trebles and one four-fold) on four selections in different events. At least two selections must be successful to get a return.

Yard A trainer's premises from where racehorses are trained.

Yearling A foal from 1 January to 31 December of the year following its birth.

Yielding Irish term to describe racecourse going that is soft.